Kevin Crossley-Holland has written eight collections of poetry. His translations from Anglo-Saxon are gathered in *The Anglo-Saxon World*, *The Exeter Book Riddles* and *Beowulf*, and he is the author of *The Penguin Book of Norse Myths*. Last year, he published his moving memoir of childhood, *The Hidden Roads*, praised by Rowan Williams as 'A lovely, poignant book, not wasting a word and evoking place in a deep way.'

His books for children include retellings of traditional tales as well as the *Arthur* trilogy (translated into twenty-four languages) and *Gatty's Tale*, and have been awarded the Carnegie Medal and the Guardian Children's Fiction Prize. The first of his Viking Sagas, *Bracelet Bones*, was published earlier this year.

He has worked with many composers, including Sir Arthur Bliss, William Mathias, Nicola LeFanu, Lynne Plowman, Giles Swayne and Bernard Hughes; with Ivan Cutting he co-authored *The Wuffings*, a play about the birth of East Anglia; and with Lawrence Sail he edited two anthologies, *Light Unlocked: Christmas Card Poems* and *The New Exeter Book of Riddles*. He has collaborated with the photographer John Fudgecoe and the artists John Lawrence, James Dodds and Charles Keeping, and joined forces with Norman Ackroyd to produce *Moored Man*, a cycle of north Norfolk poems, watercolours and etchings.

Kevin Crossley-Holland is a Fellow of the Royal Society of Literature, and patron of the Society for Storytelling and of the European Storytelling Archive. He is an Honorary Fellow of St Edmund Hall, Oxford.

Poetry by the same author

Kevin Crossley-Holland

The Mountains
of Norfolk

New and Selected Poems

ENITHARMON PRESS

First published in 2011
by Enitharmon Press
26B Caversham Road
London NW5 2DU

www.enitharmon.co.uk

Distributed in the UK by
Central Books
99 Wallis Road
London E9 5LN

Distributed in the USA and Canada
by Dufour Editions Inc.
PO Box 7, Chester Springs
PA 19425, USA

ISBN: 978-1-907587-09-2

Enitharmon Press gratefully acknowledges the
financial support of Arts Council England.

British Library Cataloguing-in-Publication Data.
A catalogue record for this book is available
from the British Library.

Designed in Albertina by Libanus Press
and printed in England by
Antony Rowe Ltd

NOTE AND ACKNOWLEDGEMENTS

In making this selection, I have restored a number of poems from earlier collections omitted from my *Selected Poems*, published ten years ago.

The sequence of poems 'Moored Man' was first published by Enitharmon Editions as an artist's book with etchings and water-colours by Norman Ackroyd, and I'm most grateful to Ronald Blythe for evaluating it. Norman Ackroyd has also generously allowed me to use his fine watercolour of Scolt Head for the cover of this new book.

'In the Window-Seat', 'Salt-Brambles' and 'The Patient Wife' were first published in *Ambit*. 'At the Joch' was first printed in *Poetry and Audience*, 'Hammershøi' in *Poetry Review*, 'Yearlings' in *The Rialto*, 'Breathless' in *Smith's Knoll*, 'Chuntering' in *Smoke*, 'Rising' in *Temenos Academy Review* and 'Bernard' in *Tideline*.

'Hubbub' was written at the invitation of Jack and Linda Hoechsler and, in a setting by Giles Swayne, was first performed in September 2010 by the choir of Clare College, Cambridge conducted by Tim Brown.

CONTENTS

NEW POEMS

THE RAIN-GIVER

DAY

The sky's visor opened: there was a face,
Immense and undefined, bearing down on you
Who staggered round the stairhead, dangerously,
Looking up at the glass, and through the glass,
At the clouds crossing. And you were awed
As the face dissolved in water streams,
Then reformed, better defined, still blurred
By the uneven, eighteenth-century glass.
This I saw, precarious on the cracking slates,
Bucket in hand, cleaning the cupola.
And you called out, a loud, demanding shout,
Perhaps to cover your uncertainty.
You shrank when I replied with reassurances;
My disembodied call reverberated
Down the flights, died shivering in the hall.

NIGHT

There was thunder, somewhere, a long way off
And never nearer, like a gong struck lightly.
Dusk came; you could hear it no longer,
And the rain came, softly – a shadow stealing up
Then rapping at the cupola. 'Rain,'
You called, 'rainrain.' We stood on the stairhead,
Peering into the black, topless hole.
You know he lives there, though you cannot see him.
He hides from you behind a mask of darkness,
The powerful one, the rain-giver. He stands
Behind the panes and smacks them with his hands;
You laugh and acknowledge him again and again.
And now you call out for my attention,
Point out the dark stain which has seeped
Through the cupola, trickles down the wall.

THE WALL

I am a desolate wall, accumulator of lichen.
Men made me with flint chippings and, fickle as always,
ignored me; time did not ignore them.
My business is to divide things: the green ribbons
of grass from the streams of macadam; the kitchen gardens
from the marsh acres, garish with sea-lavender;
the copses of ilex and pine from the North Sea,
the bludgeoning waves of salt water where seabirds play.
I stand grey under the East Anglian sky,
glint when the occasional sun opens its eye.

My business is to divide things, my duty to protect.
I am unrepaired; men neglect me at their own risk.
Time takes me in mouthfuls. The teeth of the frost
bit into my body here; here my mortar crumbles.
The wind rubs salt into every wound.
Elsewhere I am overgrown with insidious ivy;
it wound its arms around me only to strangle me.

Relentless, the sea rolls down from the Pole.
It levelled the dunes last year, removed the marram grass,
clashed its steel cymbals over the marsh and macadam.
It attacked me and undermined me; I sway
like a drunkard now; yet it could not gash me
with its gleaming scythes, it was not strong enough.
I stand, sad, and stare at all this estate,
the lawns, the kitchen gardens, copses garrulous
in the wind. I carefully listen, listen and wait
for the fierce outsider to force his way in.

DUSK, BURNHAM-OVERY-STAITHE

The blue hour ends, this world
floats on a great stillness.

I only guess where marsh
finishes and sky begins,

each grows out of the other.
In the creek a slip

of water gleams. Rowboats
bob and swing above the mud,

the barnacled and broken
ribs of Old Stoker's boat.

A wedge of gulls rustles
overhead, and for a moment

the water notices them.
Such calm is some prelude.

Then across the marsh it comes,
the sound as of an endless

train in a distant cutting,
the god working his way back,

butting and shunting,
reclaiming his territory.

This world's his soundbox now;
in the stillness he still moves.

Anything could happen.

CONFESSIONAL

I come once more to this terrible place.
As it was it is, each stone and each face

Unchanged, making an index of the change
In me. Everything here was arranged

Long ago; the wind, raking from the north,
Saw to that and sees to it. In the hearth

Coals glow and the ash flies early and late;
Every face is ruckled, sands corrugate;

Inland, those superstitious hawthorn trees
Strain away from the wind and heckled seas.

Yet I come. Here alone I cannot sham.
The place insists that I know who I am.

Elemental trinity – earth, air, sea –
Harshly advocate my humility:

You are bigoted, over ambitious,
You are proud, you salute the meretricious.

Then I have altered this much with the years:
That I need more to admit my errors,

From fear, and a longing not to be blind;
So I am scoured by the unchanging wind,

And rid again of some superfluity
By that force uninterested in me.

And I can go, prepared for the possible;
Dream and bone set out from the confessional.

A LINDISFARNE TOMBSTONE
for Eric Elstob

1

Norsemen storm the cells:
The hive ablaze; sluice of blood,
Garnet-bright, under sword and axe;
The golden comb iron reaps;
A knot of monks drone Pax Pax
By candles' light; wax weeps.

A furore Normanorum, libera nos, Domine.

2

Two monks crooked in prayer:
Cuthbert incorrupt and unscathed;
A good haul from Bee Hill;
Quick requital for slaughter;
Freedom from shadows still
Shrithing over the minds' water.

A furore Normanorum, libera nos, Domine.

THE ISLAND

Seven days, seven nights in a place of stone:
Atlantic anvil where winds and water hone
Men to what they are, long bundles of bone.

Seven days, seven nights in a place of stone
Where each man learns he is at last alone,
So quickly comes to love, forgive, condone.

Seven days, seven nights in a place of stone.
Saffron flowers in the fissures are soon grown
To all they can become: each one its own

Spirit's song, momentary wild laughter thrown
Against grey walls, the grey sky, the grey sea.

THE FIRST ISLAND

There it was, the island.

Low-slung sandhills like land-waves, fettered by marram.
One hut, a dark nugget. Across the creeks gleaming like
tin, like obsidian, across the marshes almost rust,
olive, serge, fawn, purpled for a season, the island.

We shoaled on the Staithe, stared out and possessed it;
children who collar half the world with a shout, and
share it in a secret.

Old men sat on a form lodged against the wall.
Of course we did not ask. We knew. They were too old.

There it was, and at times not there. Atmosphere
thickened, earth and air and water became one lung;
we were in a wilderness.

In a coat of changing colours it awaited us. In the
calm seas of our sleep it always loomed, always ahead.
We woke, instantly awake. As if we never had been
tired, and all things were possible.

So the boat came for us. The island stretched out to
us and we took it for granted. And no one asked by
which creeks we had come or could return.

PETAL AND STONE

An old antithesis: petal and stone.
There were anemones near that valley site,
Furled against such freezing wind. They alone
Looked living in that mottled place – blood-bright.

She dropped to her knees by a brilliant small
Colony, carefully selected one,
And leaned back against a rock. That was all
It seemed, but it could have been a lion:

Only the torso, and that mauled by time,
But still the defiant cold lord of the land.
She stretched out against it, so tender, feline:
The flower had opened to wilt in her hand.

BEHIND HIM

The old man peered into the mirror:
He saw the poppies there and picked them.
He peered into the mirror,
He knew there was something just behind him
If only he could fathom it.
He turned round; that was no good.
The old man peered into the mirror:

Sweet crushed cradling grass,
Green light white between the leaves
Of elm trees tall and toppling.
The old man raised his arms
But he knew there was something else.
He turned round; that was no good.
A pool of still water he bathed his hands in,
Mist rising and falling, falling,
A sea of blind iris.

THE DREAM-HOUSE

My eyes are sore. They sting with my own salt.
This day I have been the fetch of the sea.

Those shapes are round and kind yet fast as rocks.
What are their names? I must think of their names.

They speak firm words in soft ways. I like it
When they speak, and when they sit with no words.

Look at him, then. Look at him. John, John, John,
Once more a small wee boy, old bag of bones.

At your head the wax burns and Christ stares down
From the Cross. It is all just as it was

When you were a child and I was a child,
Each on our own in the long dark. You seem

To sleep as I would. No, it is not that,
Or it is that but more than that. I look

And you are not tired and not sad; you are calm
As the swell of the slow deep sea in June.

All you were in your time smiles as you meet,
Like a long lost friend, the end of all time.

First James now John in six months. So I am
The last one. Soon he must leave his clean sheets,

His bed, for the press of earth on the lid.
What are these? Why do I cry tears once more?

My sleeve is as rough as a tom cat's tongue.
Do not look at me. I am troughs and waves.

What is that noise? That noise? A gale of laughs
From young men and girls that sit at the hearth.

Where do they think they are? This is a wake,
Not a dance hall. They grin and nudge and wink.

John, John, John, this is your wake. I will stand
When I can and throw the pack of them out.

This is your wake, not a dance hall. No, no,
I am wrong. Let it be as it should be.

Let there be smoke from pipes, the games and songs.
They are his friends who chose to come and choose

To stay as long as this long night. We were
The same, quick in our words and ways, our blood.

What is the time? The priest will come with prayers,
Then the day with wind, tears. It will be done.

Your will be done. John, John, John, I will clean
The lamp in your room as if you were here.

VISION

Watch me if you want to.
I'm as shifty as a daddy-long-legs
on a polished pane.
You are where I was
and you will never catch me.

Why do you never tire of me?
Is it simply that I am
always beyond you,
all but indiscernible,
air trembling before rain?

I am your pursuit,
your thirst, your one thought;
only the mirage
that only will refresh you.
Watch me (if you want to).

GLUM'S WARPING

Remember the way west up over Hrafkel's land?
The path string-thin, sorry as a sheep run,
Out of his shieling and into Shut Wood?
Men called that the mossmen's track.
Year after year we used to climb it,
Pairs or small groups strapped with panniers,
Until the troll-terror... True?
Listen to this, and you will not need ask.
See my old hand: with hammer-sign
And sign of cross I swear it so.

Glum Gunnarson ganged up with me.
(He turned many heads, handsome,
Fearless, eager for fame. On his account
Married women wished they were widows
And single girls slept uncertainly.)
It was July. Just after dawn
We met and, chewing mastic, made
Our way through Shut Wood. After that,
A short cut beneath Shouting Cliff
And so we reached the moss rafts under the glacier.

For ten seconds I'd turned my back,
Having a piss. Imagine this:
Glum was straining every sinew, racing
Up towards the glacier; and there, ghastly
On an icy spur, sat a troll-
Woman, waiting. Ugly and gigantic,
With huge, crossed hands she beckoned him.
'Glum! Glum!' I yelled. No good.
He buried himself in her breast without a backward glance
And she loped away over the ice.

The dear man was mourned in Blafell,
He was missed at the Allthing. People thought
The ogress might rub him with ointment – as one
Rubbed Thorvald thirty years ago –
And stretch him, and shout into his ears,
Trying to turn him into a troll.
And no grey-haired man at all gave Glum
The least change of escaping the giantess
If he had licked her ladle; they said
His fate would be to fare the fells always.

Summer, autumn, the usual antiphon,
Then the dirge of winter: we lit candles
For Glum, hopeless, yet grim and hoping.

The next spring two shepherds –
I was out from Iceland, south over sea –
They found Glum at the foot of the glacier,
Tatterdemalion. With cries and tears
They greeted him. One asked, 'Are you still man?'
The other: 'What do you believe in?'
'God,' growled Glum and at once stumped away.

Next summer solstice I saw him myself,
My friend, gruesome, with a growth of hair for clothing.
Savagely he scowled as he shrithed from the glacier;
He was so surly, a fimbul-fambi with no tongue,
And yet he stayed by me – what was he thinking?
Of girls with fair tresses, friendship in Blafell?
'Glum Gunnarson, what do you believe in?'
'Trunt, Trunt,' he grunted. 'Trunt,
And the trolls in the fells.' He guffawed and stalked off,
Gone for ever. That is the end of the story.

The rudiments of this poem derive from a story collected by Jón Arnason in The
Folktales and Fairy Tales of Iceland.

THE MONK'S REFLECTIONS

Too much consistency: at last I dared
Kick the comfortable restraints, the bells'
Gentle hubbub, fraternal silences,
Dispersals and reunions. All our
Observances, the Rule, had become soft
With regiment and custom: time to change.

This is what I tried to think, partly thought,
Repeated so often because I had

Still to convince myself; then I kissed all
My brethren and under my skin hurried
To the spines of breakers, growling and grey-green,
The bucking ocean. My heart was aching.

I wanted to negotiate my own
Way to heaven, a crash course hazardous
With iceberg and whale: glass mountains that sing
Of how they will mother what mothered them;
Fastitocalon, apparent island
Who sinks the unwary anchored on him.

So for love I sailed north. Guided by God,
Wind-guardian, I left the secret glades,
The salmon streams, and crossed the bitter sea
Until I was driven to this loveless
Extremity. And, even now, I do
Not know the name of this icy cauldron.

This is my cell of the senses: time counts
In here and I count it – for each day
One stroke on that stripped log, and each full moon
A striation. My knife itself is pared
Like bark or rind. Five years, and rows of days . . .
Only God can tell how many longer.

And in that small cell, with its sky-ceiling,
I celebrate the offices. *O God,*
Seven times a day do I praise thee. At
Midnight I will rise and give thanks to thee.
Between boulders I pray, and between
Prayers cultivate crops and fantasies.

For how can I forget her, Grania,
Her flaming eyes? I cannot help my dreams.
I'm a rack-wretch, even now unable

To forget her, unable to flatten
The mind's fenders and remember clearly.
Even these words . . .

Your voice had to do with the bees; your eyes
Were on fire. Do you think of that green glade,
The sun behind the leaves, the leafy bed?
Do you think about those oaths, made and broken?
How did you look? And how do you look now?
Your oval face I saw in every face,

From which, after all, there is no escape?
I thought it was right to come, and maybe
It was right, but I should have explained it.
At least that. Now I cannot undo it,
And even if in time you understood,
You will have branded me lover-coward.

Life around me as my body withers:
The timeless stream of all things that are born
And do die, all children of one mother.
I am peaceful at times, incorporate;
Then the sublime whole shatters, and each part
Translates her, it embodies Grania.

I single out a sweet pattern of stars,
Her configuration in the chill air,
She is that remote light on the mountain,
This brown-eyed flower. Each is an ambush,
A torturer divine; for though I live –
In labour, prayer, shifting dream – I seem now

To live only through these incarnations.

CHILDREN IN THE CHERRY TREE

They perch in the cherry tree – two fledglings
Not quite hidden, gigglers in the dusk, hatching a plan.
The tree begins to shake them. It is not laughing,
It groans, its limbs beat slowly like prehistoric wings
And skin-soft leaves, yellow and pink and red, cascade.

So high and so cold, the tree now such a stranger.

Peering out from their eyrie, and down through the web
Of branches, the silent high-riders hear shouts
In their throats. Their colours are lowered, dashes
Of scarlet and white legging it down as light fails,
As darkness lopes along the waiting blue hills.

GRANDMOTHER'S FOOTSTEPS

No to the birds no to the flowers no to the sprinkler
All washing the garden with soft water colours
As the sun goes down. No to the friends presents
Cakes candles laughter. It is as if they were not
And had never been. Alone she stands at one end
Of the lawn facing all that does not matter
Only aware of that dark tunnel behind her.

As the shapes approach stealthy and insistent
Steps of the smilers silent and murderous
She clenches her teeth her fists her limbs almost lock
And she stares into the darkness. But there
Is still so much she can do with sheer vigilance

For so long for as long as her mind body her own will
Do not work against her. There! And there!
In her straightjacket she jerks twists round
'You and you and Ivan you Sally and you
I saw you moving almost all of you.'
Laughing they troop back to the starting-line most of them
But no not all those other ones how long will it be?

The garden is hushed at sundown it is breathless
And blooms burn to ashes. She knows they must get her
In the end they must let that be soon now.
As if only it were not a deadly serious game
How gladly she would let the first last shape touch her
And even embrace it weeping from such weariness
And relief. But as it is she turns and turns . . .

NIGHT FLIGHT OUT OF ENGLAND

Already alien: a shining pictograph I can't decipher.
And then a gold settlement not quite as regular
As polka dots; solitaries like stars fallen,
Or just night lights on landings, so dim and forever;
Spokes shooting from a hub that's greenish and ethereal,
Tangents, rhomboids, all that matter made material;
And then the last arrested flash, a scimitar of light,
And I am in the dark; and rising still, still rising,
Quickening to prospects beyond the darkness, look back
Almost lovingly at the land's concealed depressions,
Those seeming patterns, the whole bright bag of tricks.

AN APPROACH TO THE MARSH

The rope is almost paid out here. Bawdeswell
and the ghost of its foul reeve left to stew,
I drive down cool green naves, and soon the lanes
begin to ripple. More pilgrims are shuffled off
to the shrine at Walsingham, and that is an end
to the firm ground of conviction. This is no man's land
that never belongs to earth or sea entirely:
now the flowing barley hemmed by screaming poppies,
a gull perched on a salt-rusted ploughshare
and a gull, a litter of blood-tarred feathers,
festering. A veil of butterflies, opalescent,
dips and quivers and rises, and I come to where
there is no going beyond.
            Marsh, mud, shifting sand,
creeks sinuous and shining, they look sucked
and rendered almost certain by the sun;
but now and then, and for no evident reason,
rigging yaps, or seabirds shriek at what we cannot
even see, or the sea broadcasts over the marsh . . .
This bleached boat, that dabber, those children
gathering samphire, leaping over sun-crazed pulks:
the staithe today rests on its August oars;
hard light gives an edge to all that's apparent,
where nothing is what it seems or not for long.

MOSQUITO

Silent fizzer, sting white in the sunlight,
arrowing through air-tides –
                              no sooner said
than you suspect and circle a target
or drift sideways into shadow, unassailable.

A splinter of man's own irritation,
you were here in the beginning,
grinding your teeth.
                              Not much more
than your own appetite, you pick locks
as you please and are skilled at escape.
You weave out of corners, fade before lunges,
Houdini of the darkening straits.

But you come back for more. Disengagement
cannot be your tactic.
                              This is a war-game
and ends only with blood's scintilla.
Or no, does not end at all. Abroad,
and under the fan: the shades of your autograph
walk all day across my prickling skin.

SOUTH-WEST MONSOON

The eyelids of a dreaming man; the subtle
Swift movement of a trout into shadow
Or is it the white shift of water itself.
Ripple and flicker, flicker and ripple,
The far-off lightning makes its connections

In the skull. It is very peaceful.
There are no reports. As if the war
Were conducted tonight on some other front.

> As it was then . . . a malt in my hand
> (Especially shipped for the English Club),
> A trichinopoli, and a verandah,
> Not an infernal pink-and-muggy room.
> Boys waiting in the shadows . . . damn them!
> They even move like shadows of themselves.
> I'll sit in my cane before this flickering
> Screen, prepared for what may not ever come.

Dazed brass gleams like a fallen moon:
A girl with a waterpot on her head
Walks her liquid walk up the rustling road,
She is sizing the world under her soles.
If she stopped to think, she could tell
Nothing has changed since the beginning.
Aching limbs, sweet water from the well,
Aching limbs ... A mongrel howls ...

> Every four seconds the needle dances
> And the scape is scalded. Plantains leap
> Out of Dravidian dark, the compound of huts,
> The coarse thatching of coconut palm, old men
> At the thresholds. No one moves.
> No one has ever moved. At times like this
> You could stuff the whole bloody scene
> And no one would know the difference.

The cool tones of the wind's announcement:
Then rain, sheet rain, smacks the glazed face
Of the hotel. In a hundred frames
The sheet glass rocks and holds. The world contracts.
Beyond the panes not even one smear of light,
A kerosene star; the whole compound wiped out.

A Noah's Ark full of grateful prisoners,
The hotel buckets into the darkness.

Yes, I remember ... the bluster, the dark wave
That hoisted us on to its shoulder.
'Batten the hatches! Batten the hatches!'
Nothing to do but sit and sweat it out,
The lizards watching the dancing mosquitoes;
The eyes of the boys, molten, secretive;
The winking eye of malt; eye of the storm;
The bungalow bleared, a drowning eye.

Seep and trickle first, pool under the window,
A wound superficial and easily dressed;
But then water wells under the crooked door
And boys hurry in with cloths and containers.
The breach is made, though, the body imperilled.
Fabric and form, what is not at risk
In time of these rains that hammer at the house
Of the active man, the house of the head?

NEENIE
in memory of F. I. M. Crossley-Holland

Under the cowl, out on Scolt Head
The swell and swash are inching their way back.
The water picks up pebbles, razor shells,
Birds' small bleached bones and witches' purses;
It toys with them, cries over them,
And the legendary wave embraces them.

The tide returning: each wave and whisker,
Everything forged into one force,
A fusion with one meaning and purpose.
But I think you are going further,
Ancient shuffler, at the fire now, flushed
By this last blaze before going to bed.

Out of the dark they come at a knobbled wave,
Processions unblemished and undeterred
By time's strictures. Here is the hall
At Oakwell: *The chimney always roars like this;*
Frank is still up in the organ gallery,
Puffing his cigar, blowing out another hymn.

The wind, more wind, and the cottage
Rocks like a boat, quite safe, out at sea.
Remember the train we took up to Wengen
When you were six and I was sixty?
It rocks, nurse, it rocks. I love this nursery.
Kevin, have you met my pregnant sister?

And now there is rain, ripping against the window
(Long since painted into its frame)
Behind the curtain of faded red velvet.
What will become of the passion flowers?
Still, the borders of this tapestry are teeming
With forget-me-knots. I had three proposals . . .

It goes on and on. You make associations
As children and poets do, bony fingers
Clamped to the sill now, eyes watering:
Not only the tide flowing and gathering up
As it goes, not only time defused,
But for itself a parade of whatever mattered

And for whatever reason, a statement
Risen clear of interest and argument.
I listen and think you are telling something
Greater than its parts, a breath and sum
Of life itself, the ego dispossessed.
Grandmother, sleep, and sleep in peace.

A WREATH
for Edmund

The furled cypress contains it. The breathless yew. Hulks of elms all
over England.

A trail of shadows, everywhere, in the oblique sunlight. Who does not
accept them? Who is not even grateful for them?

But when the bud . . .

Not one sound can be undone. It is part of the harmony of the gong.

Look at the water. It sways, catches chips of light, flashes, sways.

Yet snared by time, all of us, that part of us . . .

Not one stone, one leaf, one flame, one breath. Whatever begins is
eternal.

Where he lies now a moonstone lies, one with flint and chert and every
granule of earth.

And the darkness comprehendeth it not . . .

A moonstone on her throbbing hand. Light in the stone, life's pointer.
Brother of the hawthorn, the wood-anemone, the breathing
iridescent universe.

from WATERSLAIN

On the Dyke

Years back,
still on the first green leg
a boy walks side by side
with his fair-haired younger sister.

How earnestly they talk!
How little they miss of the world
between us!
They've ambushed almost half the tribe out
in the slant sunlight!

I can hear their voices
far off and very clear . . .
For as long as I watch
they come on towards me.

Laddie first, riddling
mussels on the Hard,
and Fred stepping out with a good-looking dame,

then down to the dark pools tepid
and chill,
Diz dabbing for her supper.

They corner St Vitus,
eager for spoils,
advance on laughing Agnes . . .
pass up luckless Bodge.

At the first elbow
they begin to frisk and shout;
they scramble, somersault,
vault this whole embankment

first breached and sandbagged in the Great Flood,
forgetful once more
under wild rose, silverweed, spurrey.

A wave from the Warden
and they're out on their own again . . .

It's afternoon and slant
and of all places in England
I walk here today,
this lifeline and frontier at Waterslain.

Mrs Riches

A screw of peardrops
ready for each milk-white child
arrived late
last night from miles inland.

Through the gloom
in that low-slung stockpiled room
proofed with boxes
her growl conspiratorial:

'Owd Billie's gone.'
'Sin what Vic ploughed up?'
'McCullough's buyin' into Hunst'n.'
'Vitus found a walrus.'

And that once, horrified,
leaning right across her counter:

'Foive at Heacham
and Wilkie's houseboat wedged
up East Harbour Way

and that owd MTB
dumped on the quay at Wells
and sin the sandbags
and first owd Arthur knew was water
through his keyhole . . .'

No tale, not even this,
quite all told
in this spiced corner of paradise,
the bell always being rung.

Diz

Easterlies have sandpapered her larynx.

Webbed fingers, webbed feet:
last child of a seal family.

There is a blue flame at her hearth, blue
mussels at her board.
Her bath is the gannet's bath.

Rents one windy room at the top of a ladder.
Reeks of kelp.

'Suffer the little children,' she barks
and the children – all the little ones –
are enchanted.

She has stroked through the indigo of
Dead Man's Pool
and returned with secrets.

They slip their moorings. They
tack towards her glittering eyes.

Billy

Every year a new draft,
this buoy replanted, this groyne half-
dismantled, the Cockle Path patched up,
and the Mouth itself narrower, wider ...
For how, since Ararat,
can earth or sea ever be satisfied?

He knows these creeks inch by inch,
their silt and shining, their dark complexities,
and when to shoulder the *Rosemary* into action,
veterans both of Dunkirk.

'C'mon, then, me bootie!'
Infirm and elderly and eager young
he hands from jetty into bows,
a salt shepherd
gentling doubts, winking at such high hopes.

Eyes pale blue, say lace agate,
as the North Sea never is.
Eyes that on a clear day
see over a thousand scrolls
to the end of the world.

Diddakoi

The wheel of swart water
noiseless
that whirls above the dead, retracted eye;

and the spiked piers that never
impaled Hitler,
still hungry for landings;

the four cracked sails,
shining whore berries
and on Gun Hill the frayed red flag;

and Joan
with her duff pegs and sunset scarf –
not her light
fingers or wide hips

but the craft,
the blood,
and the patterns on the sands
before the tide absolved them:

in the same black breath
speak them.

Bodge

He is their cracked mirror
and the boys don't like what they can see:

the work of a cruel caricaturist –
a boneless dumpling
who grins too long and blubs too much,
upper lip always damp with snot or sweat.

Elbowed out of their secret councils,
their expeditions
cockling, crabbing, cycling the lost lanes,
he teaches them their cruelty.

And on the beach alone
under the sky's awnings,
shy of the sea's claws,
he gives back their sense of loneliness.

Pink and fluttering and maimed:
seldom, they discover, can the tongue sing
just what the heart means.

Bloated windsock, crumpling.

Only later do they come on
the Christian virtues.
In the mirror each face suffers a smile.

Shuck

From saucer pulks
where pale light lingers longest
we made his eyes.

In this seedbed only think:
Dead Hands wave, Things worm,
marsh lights flicker.

We made his blood from arteries
obsidian in the moonlight,
his hair from shaggy sea-purslane.
His chains are chains of marsh mist.

Skriker, Hooter, Fenrir:
these are his blood-brothers.
We gave him the howl of wind
carried from Siberia.

And witnesses?
With terror or with damp black
earth, one way or another
he stops every mouth.

Beachcomber

Faithful as a wordfisher,
there he goes, old magpie of the foreshore!
Face chafed and chapped like driftwood.

Parcelled shapeless against
winds straight off the icecap
but look! agile even so, jumpy as a tick,
quick in his pickings.

Scoofs along the tideline scurf,
his oily sack full of consonants:
hunks of wax,
and seacoal, rubber ballast, cork,
sodden gleanings.

And swinging in that shoe-bag hitched
to his broad belt?
Ah! In there, sunlight and amber moonlight,
emerald and zinc and shell-pink,
Aegir's vowels.

The Great Painter

Though his spirit
possesses that house as surely as
violet shades course through the creek,
shutters blind the windows from month to month
and salt cancers the royal blue.

He has escaped to sweets
at St Columb, and Paris and Provence,
a plump indulgent wavelength
of pink and crimson, viridian, ultramarine.

The lines here are too Lutheran:
flat-chested dunes,
the ruled horizontals of marsh and ocean.

Too near the bone!
He shuddered when the wind's mouth framed
its forbidding questions.

Not for him
light honed on a northern whetstone,
the burning ice of aurora borealis;
nor was he the first to flinch
at this ruthless incandescence,
too cutting even for Crome and Cotman,
still awaiting a master.

Caretaker

When the tarmac's in a sweat
and Poker's field is waterslain,
his leafy books curl up like shrimps.

That serves him right.
The staithe needs life, not furriners,

only
so little life is left:
nothing but dregs up Norton Creek
once ploughed by shingle boats and whelkers,
black silt over landing stages,
a poor crop
of children unlikely to stay.

It's the same with half his class:

no thought except for Number One.
They would've pumped
not sucked
if this place were not a plaything
but their heartbeat.

Old fule!
You can squeeze his bleeding walls.
Dry, I write. *Dry*.

Local Historian
a found poem

A low flat coastline, sand and saltmarsh;
and a streak of light,
bright as fish scales . . .

Up to 100 tons, malt, coal, corn and oil-cake;
the great granaries and maltings
all converted . . .

Ceased to be
cruciform. Mutilated; mutilated;
now form the Brothercross
on the little green below the church.
Squat, crouching tightly;
the wind sweeping in from the sea . . .

Paid for destroying of Jackdaws;
Paid Gam Gregory
for spreading the mould in the churchyard;
Payd to Joseph Bobbit for a Book
which is concerned with distemper which now rages
amongst the horned cattle;
Paid for 12 Jackdoyes (jackdoyes 3 a 1d.) . . .

41

A very gruesome story:
in the year 1307
William Umphrey, chaplain, and Robert de Orleyns
boarded his ship,
bound his hands behind his back until
the blood gushed out at the nails,
imprisoned him until . . .

As a boy Horatio Nelson;
a short cut through the churchyard;
the headstones bear many names still very familiar –
Woodget, Parr, Haines, Scoles, Riches, Thompson,
   Mason . . .
Have gone; remain; in spite of; whirlpools;
think; walk; rustles;
windows.

Wildfowler

Seven sounds in the pallor.

The sound of the silent assassin –
a slice of white moon
between his teeth.

The sound of no-wind,
nothing but pressure in the silent frame.

Then sleeping water,
not stertorous or small-sighing,
still lost in some dark sliding dream.

The mutter on the marsh
and at once its antiphon –
Banjo's shallow breathing.

Now it comes,
the thickening of air,
the rush of wings
and passionate sky-voices:
a spring of teal,
then mallard, jinking redshank, widgeon.

The No. 4 out of the Magnum.

Great clump on the marsh, splash in the creek,
and Banjo's off !

– All before the opening
of day's intricate soundbox.

Vic

Stirs; quite delicately sips;
yawns over Friday's yellowed *Advertiser* . . .

Outside is cold as inside
is cold, wind flights over the marsh,
the walls of the sky drip
as Vic already rises,
eases himself out, pink and primed,

into the beginning –
shapes still inchoate,
pewter on oyster, seacoal on zinc.
Time never was for pondering.

Banjo far-off on the brew!
A taste of plickplack in the air!
No smell of sharp rain!
His sense of day is animal
and utterly secure.

Crossing the yard,
he gossips
with passerines in the thistle scrub;
hails and cajoles the two Suffolks
(the black gelding and chestnut mare)
into the shafts . . .

Didn't you see his wading walk?
That almost inward smile?
He is this land's stage manager –

dawn corrugator,
trawler of a thousand screaming gulls –

overseer
in the candid light
watching you for one moment
longer
than you watched him.

John

Unlike that *shiten shepherde* down the road,
his staff is duty, his smocking
self-effacement,
as if he thinks to keep his head
well down might enable his flock to win
a better view of God.

Time has not incised his face but moulded it.

After the Black Death's lapping,
the sea's recession:
oyster-men and salt-men and samphire-gatherers,
they all followed

the singing tideline,
    turned their backs on this flint hulk
    (thirty years and still unfinished)
    in the lee of the hill.

    Not lost in the mind's labyrinth –
    unmoved by the sophistry of disputation,
    the ecstasy of mystics –
    but always on the road, spinning
    round his parishes 'held in plurality',
    year by year he has sought
    to narrow that old gap between
    man and God.

    His slow smile is part of God's promise.

    'Listen' he says. 'Only listen.'
    He listens in prayer,
    as vacant as his beaten church
    circled by spirits of wind.
    He listens to the Word –
    King James' tidal cadences
    that follow the heart's contours.

    There was a man sent from God . . .

Miss McQueen

Gong Lane and greengages:
this morning in the orchard
I coached myself and coaxed myself
to walk alone
again:

application gets you so far.
Could've! Should've!

I never realized.
Sometime mistress of parabola and paradox,
almost finished, schooling cabbages.

This one body . . .

And now you bring me
flagrant poppies

and yes I know
John will come with communion later.

Reproofs! Consolations!
When all I see
are splayed legs, still coltish,
eyes bright in their bone stoups,
one last refusal.

Laddie

King
of the small pool.
Trooper, tussler, accruer, custodian.

Watchful and terse
as the luminous cat-tide rises
and *Duck* and *Golden* swing
then straighten
on their anchors – his engines
fuelled
on whelks and summer passengers.

The black shingle barges: his.
The mussel lays: his.

Silvermilk slakes won by Several Order.
And when the water drops back
and drains, he tracks trespassers
with huge binoculars.

Horsewhipped at thirteen.
Brought an action against the farmer.

Rowed provisions under fire
across the Tigris.

A salty word; the snick of a smile;
in no way prodigal
but English and not to be crossed.

And now
he is watching,
holding court and watching
as this spring tide still rises,
creeps through the marsh,
floods the capillaries,

until there is such a shining
as far as far Trowland and Scolt Head,
unbroken
to the line of the sallow wave.

Tertiary

Down a lane holm-oaks
hallow, all but islanded by drifts
stocky and immaculate –
snowdrop, anemone, marguerite –
Old Agnes flourishes.

Seasoned perennial,
rubicund and rotund, always affable,

she leads pilgrims out
to the green hollow
(earth springy, then giving)
and the silent ferment sweet to the tongue,
the nipples flowing.

'Here is the canal
the poor souls row down to get provisions . . .'
Suffused with lily pads and bulrushes.

'This is the aching arch
of departure and return ...'
Grey-green with lichen, crumbling.

'And here is their Dormitory . . .'
Stones for pillows.

So very little reason
why they should not be
here, white habits, white cowls,
thronging this place.

Furriner

That rumpus on the staithe,
all that flap and hoisting
as the tide rises;
reunions at the Moorings;
coronas of light in the quiet houseboats:

you
may call it artificial,
this summer respiration;
I say the place was choking on its own silt.

On the rocks, was it?

Every month another
shell for the wind to moan in . . .

What is unnatural
is this shoal of shiny Midlanders,
traipsing and sinal.
Not ratty, we call them.

Just as it is, was it?

No, when I round the bend
in the scalding lane
and see that immense, almost-empty theatre –
breathing marsh,
signals of the sea –

I say I have reached home.

Leaving

On this tall dyke
where I have walked and watched
there was a meeting.

Under the fizzing hard blue light
you must narrow your eyes at,
generations dovetailed
and half the village quickened:

gossip's sharp spindrift first,
then those considerations that seldom
trouble children – dark tides
tugging at every anchorage in the creek.

It grew late . . .

It was my own children
leaped from me,
looking in all directions.
They surge down this lifeline
here and now
towards the gold ramparts
and the skirling sea,

and still, high over them and me
and the sea-acres, the land-acres,
the gulls criss-cross
like stitches, like nets, like arguments,
like love.

WOMAN SORTING REDCURRANTS

Her back is still straight but
her eyes are bleeding.
Through the honeysuckle trellis
where she sits and sorts
swarm the domestic atrocities.

Again and again she tells
their names and their names
do not control them . . .

This sweetness is almost
unendurable. With her pale
wrist she dabs at her eyes;
unheard, the perfect drops
patter into the kitchen chalice.

THE GUARDIAN TREE

Unlike that manor oak
in Northamptonshire
it did not climb within our walls,
right-angle with the roofbeam,
and overhead explode
into a flurry of leaves.

Out in Iceland
on the howling farmsteads
solitary trees graze outer walls,
they lean against each other
in mutual dependence.
It was not like these.

No dragon gnawing at its root,
no eagle in its high uneasy branches,
no deer, no goats
tearing at the green shoots:
nothing fabulous or universal.
No fructifer, no seductive
sweet dew on its leaves,
no spirit-ladder.

We seldom gave it thought:
a guess at its age
and surprise it survived a bomb
meant for the Docks;
a second desultory guess
(being neither children nor trigonometrists)
at its huge reaching height;
though we fretted at its red scab, and peered
for the lost canary,
and raked and cursed and

carted off its leaves,
and once, one June evening,
we made love beneath it,
inviolate
as its green arms
waved away the world.

Not only bereft now;
abandoned, as children by a mother.
It was our cap of happiness,
rough-tongued and embracing,
our pennyplain guardian tree,
rooted in earth but
free of doubt and cause and argument,
rising above change.

PREPARATORY SCHOOL

Licker Lonsdale could tap dance.
His hot eyes stripped us
naked so Murdoch the Mole used to burrow
beneath his blankets before
lights out.

Unlike Henry's generous backhanders
(purple stripes on the badge of the buttocks),
Grummet's half-nelsons brought me to my knees.

Holland had some pox and was nicknamed Morbus.
He left the term before I came;
thus I was accorded his name.

Hymn 25 in the *Public School Hymnbook*.
The day thou gavest, Lord,
the one day between now and half-term.
My tears lolloped on to the page.

Coronation Week, Sunday sweet shop,
lashing Henry's horrible daughter
to the crumbling Wellingtonia...

And up the usual decrepit drive,
past mature trees
and the scoreboard showing the whole team
out for 13,

I listen to the silence of your preparation
for the mad dash
past the vulturine crucifix
into the gloom,

then angrily reason with myself
all the way from Otford west into Dorset
watching your reflection
in the mirror
dissolve.

HAPPY BIRTHDAY
for Dominic at 16

How do you do, bone-house?
Here's another stepping-stone
on this risky journey –
another pause for understandings:

three pawns are worth more
than a bishop: the more I give,
the more I have to give;
no perspective without humour;

panache wins admirers; to act,
always to be my own audience;
language ties and language cuts,
mightier than Excalibur.

You will bother to read this
and take issue with it
one way or another
almost as a matter of principle.

You have a sort of spiky grace,
like a conker in its armour,
a crocketed spire, the elbows
and knees of the contrary sea.

Happy birthday, bone-house!
Here's another stepping-stone
on this risky journey –
another pause for understandings:

remember the child I'm leaving;
work against small wars;
today colours tomorrow; I will
not miss the boat to the stars.

ORKNEY GIRLS

1   *Girls at Skara Brae*

The place is a hiss.
          The cells
and passages and womb-houses, runes
of sandstone under their turf skin,
all of them defused, bleached
into static.
         Turn your back
on the usual slop and clout
and the summer blandishments
winking in the meadow.
Then enter,
listen . . .
        In the white wave
are the hiccups and polyps
and such subtle modulations
the heart decodes.
         Nothing singular,
but in this sunken room
amongst dresser, hearth and cot,
shafted by sunlight, repossessed
after five thousand winters,
this persistent broken
singing:
      Spring and a necklace . . .
scattered seed . . . now and here
and now . . . all our ripening.

2   *The Girl at Gurness*

I become little more than a voice:
a bruck of bones earth-fingered,
all unravelled and unlimbed
by salts and seep and vapours.

There! The whale-path to a farm
on a fiord, a girl in sunlight;
that road to the Irishman, clover
on his tongue, and the whirlpool of love,
and that is the way of the dove
to Jorsala. I have no knowledge
of where that way leads my brothers
with blooming axe and scramasax.

I am only in shadow saying,
Look at the rib of water passing –
the show of aquamarine, limpid,
and the lumpen everyday swell,
the furious spears of black-and-silver;
saying, Look at the shift of light
gilding the bare breasts of Rousay.

The wind is a wearisome impartial
scold. Think of the ways you also
took, or did not take . . .

(Mouth stopped. Two shoulder brooches.
An iron knife. Also lobster-shell,
an unbroken necklace, blushing pink-and-lilac.)

3 *Stromness Girl*

Her father's fathers came in
from the north, brewing and salty,
the women from the south and west –
violet Caithness, the concealments of Antrim,
locking the flint-grey ring.

Red ribbon in her hair, parts her lips . . .

Her subject is the smash and glimmer,
that sweep of the scythe intent
on shearing. After which there is
poor rest, no terra firma, risky footing.

Eyes lace agate. Painted shell necklace . . .

Oyster and pearl, not one wrinkle:
she tells of seeming and dissimulation,
elaborate surface tension above
the röst blood-dark and churning.

Glib. All glitter. Flashy rings . . .

Does not walk so much as slide
and swing. Wholly abandoned
to her legend, she shrieks with laughter,
collapses, sobs on any shoulder.

I am what you want only . . .

Gags first on a skuther of gutturals,
softens, sideways drifts in a mirror
of assonance. How her old story still
enthrals us. Shape-shifter
at the whirlpool that grinds men to dust.

ANGELS AT ST MARY'S

'The angels have gone'
Church Guide, Walsham-le-Willows

Up among bleached stars and suns
Are the tongues, protruding, oak pegs
Wanting their smiling high-fliers.

The fledglings heard black hints
And saw battle-lights advancing.
They conferred, they spread their wings.

Or did they become spirits of
Themselves? Angels rearranged,
Acute angles where clear sound and

Sunlight cross? They are in the air.

ON THE WAY EAST

The terminus smells of wild garlic,
The buttoned cloth is squirrel red-brown.
There are depths as black as black holes
Where the barley has been beaten down.

The caparisoned elms are alight
(Each stilled in a flood of gold fire).
Such dawdles! Standstills! The white
Skyline is lanced by a crocketed spire.

Wild roses cling to pink brick. The track
Is burning sienna. Almost, almost free!
Beyond the hectares of mangel and beet
Open silver-grey arms, stunning, the sea.

COMFORT

Who said anything about comfort?
Those syllables do not rhyme
with zinc slakes or ice-bright sky.
The sea is grinding her spears.
Up creeks and gullies, over groynes

the black tide surges
and the hag wind rides her.
In the bleak forest on the staithe
rigging clacks and chitters.

Little but memory for company,
wild geese, swans whooping,
but no urbanity no
gossip prejudice bitterness sham.
In London I dream of these harsh folds,
the sea's slam, the light's eagle eye,
and here again I draw
this place – hair-shirt, dear cloak –
around such infirmities.

from THE PAINTING ROOM

Creatures of a Landscape

The truant with his rod,
and cap on the back of his head;
the apple-face on the passing lighter;
and the lad astride the carthorse,
yoked to his destiny:

I'm looking at
the creatures of a paradise garden
they will never leave entirely.

How little will happen
in the whole span of their lives
not already present and planted.
They're almost fixed!

For them as for you and me
the ethic of work
will not be a matter of choice
or self-discovery
but almost an inheritance:
a fierce imperative decreed over their cradles
by a stern godmother.

And when we believe
that whatsoever we do or say
has moral implications,
it's only what our parents told us
and we observe each day
in the order of this land around us.

This dear, familiar, unshowy Eden!
It's the child of history.
It feeds me and I'll nourish it.

The Language of Light

I rise with the rising bell
every day of the week.
The river is my pointer
to read the landscape's book.

I'll sit and watch these willow
leaves silvered by the wind
until they are impressed
on the cool page of my mind.

And then these twisted roots
dressed with wads of sponge:
I'll watch them in this calm sun
until the shadows change.

I'll live in these meadows
and trace each variant.
It's with their light they speak
the language of the heart.

Correspondences

That's her!
So well disposed to the world:
the gaze unstopped, the kind shoulder.

But on my way here
I saw her in the cornfield:
her carriage, her smouldering mane.
She was gathering with the gleaners.

And that grave girl by the porch:
when I heard her,
soft and foggy
as a flute at the bottom of its register,
I thought for a moment . . .

She surprises me
everywhere
and I say to myself
there is no time when I have not loved her.

I can hear my own voice.
Not proving signs or symbols
but correspondences
are what I am looking for.

As I walk with the river
and hear, or think I hear,
the far, late harvest bell,
I see her

in the sweet incline of this willow,
the moist leaves. The dry whispers
of the flags are like a Greek chorus.

And here, this torso, aching and arched . . .

Ox-bow and lock and race:
there's laughter in the water
and salt in her veins . . .

That's her!
Did you see her
invested
and trailing green-and-gold chains?

Like Light that Gilds

She loves me and her love is light
like light that gilds the river's braid
when water-meadows drown in shade
and Bergholt's wrapped in rings of night.

Her guardians check, forbid and blight
and still her colours do not fade.
She loves me and her love is light
like light that gilds the river's braid.

Do they believe she has no fight?
Or think our love can be betrayed?
Shining, constant and unafraid,
she guides my hand and gilds my sight

like light that gilds the river's braid.

Quiet and Unquiet

In the lap of water
and the company of watermen:

the boatwright with peaceful hands
building the lighter
that will lift with the lock
the keeper is turning;
and the poler, all purpose and clout,
about to yell
at the fisherman dibbling for nothing much.

There is something
similar about these well-tempered men:
their calm brows and their bearing
and every line of their bodies
announce a complete want of anxiety.

As if to advertise the manual life,
or to say
the rod assuages,
or to commend the properties of water.

When I grow quiet,
and ready myself, and start to write,
I am one
of this engaged and placid company.

It's off the page and outside the frame
my mind snags.

Errant son, or telephone silent,
time short and money short:
the shadows lengthen,
everywhere the causes of indisposition.
It was the same for you.

Fisher was right:
worry hurts the stomach more than arsenic.
It soon generates nothing but itself.

And yet to celebrate
this company of watermen
at their usual stations, calm and accepting ...

I think we would agree
the presence of unquiet
quite essential,
vital as yeast.

Oak Leaf

This little gossip, silly
and still crumpled, tender
as a tongue! This lobe's twice
pierced, this mole almost amber . . .
  this one and this one

I picked it from the sapling
you planted at the gate,
now ample as a cumulus
childbearing and forthright
  this one and this one
  and the world is wide

No two hours are alike
and no two leaves on a tree.
Let me learn the singular
green lessons of the eye
  this one and this one
  and the world is wide
  this one and only

In Pursuit

Under rookwings
and the tatty crown,
under the lanes of clouds,
dove and lily and oyster in the dome,
the labours of the months proceed:

the ferryman and his mate
and the blinkered white horse in harness,
the plough, the little boat
with its nose in shadow, its oars
at this moment shipped,

all part of the same arduous story
the water reflects
and invigorates.

Observation close and continual . . .
to realize, not to feign . . .
less to inspire than inform . . .
and this pursuit
not to be looked on with blind wonder
but legitimate, scientific and mechanical.

I understand this too:
matter is deadweight
and form nothing but a shape
the breath of life makes beautiful.
Lightness and brightness.
The tint of English daylight, cool.

When Chantrey took your palette
and scumbled the whole foreground
with smears of asphaltum:
'There goes all my dew.'

In My Painting-Room

Wherever I step wherever I look
the canvas-weave is covered in blossom,
impasted with chestnut, cherry and lilac,

Queen Anne's lace and ropes of laburnum.
My galloping boys spring out of the brush;
and my girls, all gingham and sweet alyssum,

skip past the millrace's passion-and-rush;
and now my wife glances up at our home –
I'll dress her in sunlight: a loop of gold wash.

Child-willow, cloud-woman, the river's in bloom:
surge and reflection – life, resurrection –
lift their bright voices in my painting-room.

SOUNDS
for my father on his seventieth birthday

You dug the chalky soil; we blazed spring-trails
through high, sopping beechwoods; and in the shed
examined, catalogued and then displayed
quartz crystals, coins, potsherds from Bledlow Ridge,
fossils from the chalk-pit; at night I heard
you play – while you charmed babeldom I slept.

After a while I brought you drafts. I thought
the gardener and walker-in-the-rain,
the patient keeper with whom once I found
a Constantine, the music-man whose Dance
was sung in mildewed church, cathedral nave
and concert hall would know about word-spells.

You treated them with proper seriousness.
I see you at your study door, smiling,
taking the sheets; and then you close your eyes,
withdraw into that magic gloom of books,
piano, harmonisphere, preparing for
our sessions with small signs and spider-marks.

You thinned my words like seedlings. *And avoid*
long words where short suffice. (Work; will do.)
For vogue and buzz and all-too-commonplace
you wrote in almost timeless substitutes
(ex-Yeats, ex-Graves). *Revise and then revise.*
Our second thoughts strike deeper than the first.

Sometimes you mused aloud, or asked me how
my craft related to the science of sound –
abstract in this, its power akin to music.
And sound, you told me then, *includes silence.*
One part of the performance, integral . . .
I hear myself. Hear all that's left unsaid.

MAKING A RAINBOW

The children are making a rainbow

The children of Sling and Stroat
sons and daughters of the freeminers
have forgotten the scowls
they have lifted their eyes
they are all making a rainbow

Richard of York says Miss Rose
Richard of York gave battle in vain
and on the other side
of the hardboard partition

Miss Nicholas writes Roygbiv
in a cursive hand
and then on the blackboard in capitals
ROYGBIV

Red as rose petals, a whole poppy field,
embarrassment, the blood of a god…

Orange though is ugsome
all entrails and ventricles
the best of it
carrot juice and food Thor spat out

The tears of the sun,
a green sky-serpent…

Blue says Miss Nicholas says Miss Rose
on the other side of the hardboard partition
blue is blue is
the Blue Bird of Happiness

Now the *shell of a wood-louse,*
a basket of Victoria plums:
indigo is more sheen than substance

And violet last is flow and greeting
ocean's curtsy, seacoal burning,
a sky-wave like a rainbow herself

All in all one tiny girl raises
an ice-mirror to reflect the sun
and a boy begins *The first rainbow*
was made by men living before 989…
Neither of these extremists
wins much sympathy

The sweet rain ceases
the sun goes in

It is in the sky
says an earnest joker
(a *sage enfant* from the Pludds)
because if it was on the ground
you wouldn't be able to see it
and there wouldn't be any point
in having it

It is in the word
thinks Miss Nicholas thinks Miss Rose
in the word
sons and daughters rainbow children

NAMING YOU

We have not snared you
with the net of a name
we have not tamed you

you are energy the one
word that is every word
the sound of the gong

come into the garden
we will sing you
white stars green leaves

such spring-fever
the birds hop and cheep
around your sleepy head

the surge and shining
the rocking of tall trees
in the eager wind

who are you what are you
but the little sister
of this world around you

morning star and sparrow
bluebell smouldering
the attentive yew

* * *

but the dance of time
the argument of choice
fingers reach out

well the world can wait
we are disciples
and nothing is arbitrary

you are your own word
and cannot grow out of
a careless visitation

you declare yourself
smiling bubble-blower
your eyes gentian blue

lolling by the willow
your bald head askew
like a medieval saint

come home little sister
take your proper place
in this shining garden

dear daughter come home
come home we are here
and listening for your name

OENONE IN JANUARY

January 1st: Beginning

Fingers chapped, the clean year picked and scraped
to a glint. Halley's Comet a milk burr.
Over the long field silhouettes, guffaws,
resolutions. Then the boisterous wind.

January 2nd: Ages

She carts, cherishes and upbraids her dolls,
sowing the seeds of her own motherhood.
She is every age already. You look
as she sleeps: creaseless ancient Infanta.

January 3rd: Pretence

You core it and she eats the skin, the flesh
and then the hole! When she covers her eyes
she is hidden. She deceives you with pearls.
You hear her laughter in the swollen stream.

January 4th: Taming

Buttons, clips, pins – she always takes her tithe.
She drills tins and bottles. Nothing counter
passes without some question or comment.
This fierce attempt on the unwieldy world!

January 5th: Absences

Not maybes – those tassels whiskers, that lump
in the mattress tigerish – but maybe nots:
Can't see them! Can't hear them! Am I alone?
Bawling existentialist before dawn.

January 6th: Animateur

Spangles on her pane. Icicles wrist thick,
thick as ropes and candid. Dark clots knitted
up in the elms. The whole frieze in need of
its animateur. She opens one eye.

January 7th: Imagining

You smile, murmur *mouse*, think she clambers up
to share one pillow and rehearse the day . . .
Gulls circle mewing. You turn to the clock,
and it's not even time for her to wake.

January 8th: Invocation

All morning the sleet slanted in. She stripped
to the waist and donned seven necklaces.
Doily, felt-tips (heavy duty): she raised
a rose garden and entered it, singing.

January 9th: Numbers

One more, no more . . . In her reckoning, what
is ever complete? *Where has he went?*
*It's a shame they can't come both. I am three
years old; when will I be all the numbers?*

January 10th: Hair

A thousand clefs of curls. Her mother laughs
and says *corn-gold* (her own is titian).
Bright cloud, you think; grace notes of the skylark,
ocean, elixir . . . *Nope*, she says. *Ginger!*

January 11th: Half-Brother

She knows it's almost time for him to go.
Silver chatterbox, she trots at his heels,
dragoons him into last loud games. He smiles,
devoted, tolerant; a kind of god.

January 12th: Recognition

Good morning path! Oh! good morning puddle!
Blithe bubble all the way to Sunday School.
St Francis' sister, greeting one and all
as newborn and equal and integral.

January 13th: Rites

She takes your lobes between fingers and thumbs,
gently massages; rubs noses; warbles
into one ear. Close your eyes. Celebrate
the siren rites of the true Daughterhood!

January 14th: Rivals

Each used to undivided attention;
each queering the other's pitch. Carnations
blaze in the razor sunlight. Two *divas*
(old and young) glaring across their breakfasts!

January 15th: Chastening

That weal on the back of her hand your hand
inflicted, and the doleful cutting tears,
part sting, part shock, and part calculation:
you know it was right and feel quite stricken.

January 16th: Nightsounds

Uhu of the barn owl; cock pheasant's creak;
hackle and cackle; our lyric willow;
and always this ancient house, its whispers
and predictions. One listener: her heart.

January 17th: Dangers

That tinny sound as she tries out thin ice!
In its shine you see capsizes, crashes,
every kind of accident, then, far worse,
the smiling drivers . . . Take steps. And take steps.

January 18th: Joy

Lily, she thought; she thought, *tiger. And this
is my own daughter: dayspring and dancer
and gleam.* The late primrose light faded from
the little room. Still she looked; still she shone.

January 19th: Mother!

The least knock or scratch or ache and you are
supernumerary. Back to the source:
mātr, mḗtēr, mōdor, mutter, máthair . . .
She cries and reaches out. The woman smiles.

January 20th: Dog

Beau Brummel and Barnum and Loyal Sam!
He's her chief barker and mooning paleface,
her game opponent, grinning accomplice.
She tightens the leash: *Jealous! You're jealous!*

January 21st: Imitation

Wading round the room in black stilettos;
intent, loading a pipette; kneading dough,
sleeves rolled up: flatterer in rehearsal,
instinct with longing to learn, to succeed.

January 22nd: Lexicon

Why not can't I do it? Of course I can.
Slobber-de-bob! Isgusting! There's water
in frogtime. I want to read peoplest books.
I'll run you down. What colour is your talk?

January 23rd: Sunrise

You left both ladies in the pink, fingertips
at their temples. Each stone and each leaf
was locked in bristling frost; the whole circuit
of the sky down-pillows and pear-blossom.

January 24th: Rules

Playing percentage is unknown to her.
Draws you wide, kicks the chalk, always ends up
in dock and nettles. Proper anarchist,
years of markings stretched out in front of her.

January 25th: Spring?

Sunlight. Hedgerows and high-wavers all stripped,
all winter-bleached and ready to begin.
The dog waltzes over the fields. She primes
her shining pots with earth and warm gravel.

January 26th: Promises

Her rainbow segments dance; her cardboard clock
with its bold promise pulses. Poor sleeper,
turn, twitch, and twist, whisper of Horrid things.
Slowly her dove unfurls morning-white wings.

January 27th: Offenders

Her sequinned, squinting elephant exiled
on the landing is the offending book
your devoted grandmother blue-pencilled
and filleted. Each day it grows larger.

January 28th: Proposals

Hot and hectic and armed with a posse
of proposals: *pick-stickers; picklecheese;
house-of-cards; Humpty; stand-on-my-head* . . .
You, niggard, had one and only one: *bed!*

January 29th: There

There it snows. Here it always rains quiet always-rain
dropping into your skull. And there the north
and east winds blow. Here the colours hang limp.
There the rose. Here – how sharply you miss her.

January 30th: Commitment

Hide your eyes! She tears across the room, throws
herself on to the Chesterfield, face down,
enters a white shining darkness: no game,
no commitment ever more serious.

January 31st: Goodbye

The world is opening under our feet;
you stoop, sweep her up, you kiss her goodbye.
Three and already a breaker of hearts:
I won't see you ever again, will I?

DO YOU, OR I, OR ANYONE KNOW?

It comes up by the roots
                    dangling and unfortunate,
a straggler and victim on the field's margin
never quite caught up in the bruised gold tides.

The air's an intoxicant, laced with the sweetness
of the barley, and clay, and far thunder.

You shake off the chaplet of storm-flies
and, sharp as a bright stoat, bite through
the hempen stalk.
                    You're holding a wand.

A lick of lightning . . .
                    You break off one grain
and tickle it round the cradle of your palm.

It's a kingdom! First you peel away
pale-striped bullseye skin, then plain wrapping.

And now, half-a-minute later, the dark sky-growl.
The storm's still half-a-county off!
                                        The smiling cleft;
the ivory sheen; the warm grain still malleable.

You grind it and grit it. Unconvinced
of its relationship to barley-water, you spit it out.

Now the beard: one whisker. You hold the hilt
and run it smoothly between your fingers.
You rub it the wrong way and say, 'It's biting!'

Nothing the eye can see,
                          unlike the storm
gathering and sending shivers through the barley.
Later, you lift my little brass microscope
from its wooden box.
                          How you surprise my childhood!
Properly ginger, you lay the whisker on the glass tray.

I light a kitchen candle – rain-spears and thunder
drive in through the garden gate –
and fiddle with the mirror, the tube, the mirror . . .

Barba dentata: covering one eye with soft fingertips
you level your unblinking gaze.

HERE, AT THE TIDE'S TURNING

You close your eyes and see
                              the stillness of
the mullet-nibbled arteries, samphire
on the mudflats almost underwater,
and on the saltmarsh whiskers of couch-grass
twitching, waders roosting, sea-lavender
faded to ashes.

            In the dark or almost dark
shapes sit on the staithe muttering of plickplack,
and greenshanks, and zos beds;

                              a duck arrives
in a flap, late for a small pond party.

The small yard's creak and groan and lazy rap,
muffled water music.

                  One sky-streamer,
pale and half-frayed, still dreaming of colour.

Water and earth and air quite integral:
all Waterslain one sombre aquarelle.

From the beginning, and last year, this year,
you can think of no year when you have
not sat on this stub of a salt-eaten stanchion.

Dumbfounded by such tracts of marsh and sky –
the void swirled round you and pressed against you –
you've found a mercy in small stones.

This year, next year, you cannot think
of not returning: not to perch in the blue
hour on this blunt jetty, not to wait, as of right,

for the iron hour and the turning of the tide.

You cross the shillying and the shallows
and, stepping on to the marsh, enter
a wilderness.

        Quick wind works around you.

You are engulfed in a wave of blue flames.

No line that is not clear cut and severe,
nothing baroque or bogus. The voices
of young children rehearsing on the staithe
are lifted from another time.

               This is
battleground. Dark tide fills the winking pulks,
floods the mud-canyons.

        This flux, this anchorage.

Here you watch, you write, you tell the tides.
You walk clean into the possible.

PORLOCK: INTERRUPTED LIVES

Amongst these pink and grey stones,
some smooth, some dressed with ocean runes,
eleven US airmen died;
the salt has almost eaten their names.

The little copper plaque, crammed
by some loving inexperienced hand
(ten men identified and one unknown)
is no longer fastened
tight to the ashen headstone,

and quite soon the stone itself
will crack, or topple
and fall, and for several months
no one will even notice.

A pony down from the moors
nuzzles it; the glistening spoor
of a snail bandages it . . .

Nearby I see what might have been
a little shore sanctuary – a place for prayer
or else a pen for black-faced sheep –
reduced to an oblong shape,
almost no more than a shadow
amongst these dry, quite cordial stones.

I see a mound
and lumps not readily to be explained,
then all around the signs
of other lives and other times.

And where this wilderness is almost bald
I find doomed spears
of samphire irrupting and withering
and a single ragged thistle –
a purple perch
for a butterfly with clouded yellow wings;

and led on by the piping
of a small bird I cannot even see,
come upon a clump of quivering bleached campion.

I stoop and count
the white and shining petals –
ten and eleven and eleven and eleven.

THE SIGNS OF WALSHAM

I have seen the way in. Rightangles and rubber swerves
and deep scummy ditches. I have seen the puzzle on the
palimpsest: the forest of elm and ash, the watering
places.

I have seen the green women, all very elegant, very
particular, trilling in forever light painted in tempera.

I have seen matriarchs who buried their husbands. The
rectitude of pit-props; last survivors. Dispensers of
pullets' eggs and grace-and-favour houses.

Also the old snorters, beady, broad and blunt. I have
seen their terrible horizons.

A woman drifted, she died while spring skipped outside
her window. A newborn baby lolled in the shadow
of the yew tree. I have seen them.

I have seen tides: exiles from collapses and sagging
thatches, shoals of children, the lissom baby-sitters.
Also the old soaks, looking meaningful; buzzing
weekenders; nasal upstarts aspiring to jacuzzis.

I have seen the crusader who lost his name his date and
the crant for poor Mary who lost her heart and died. I
have seen the tradesmen hiding in the wall, the leftover
smiles of oak angels.

I have seen lists of sponsors and meringue-makers,
paragraphs of small type concerning covenants.

Every eighth minute the Bangalore Bomber. The light
plane stoops with its deadly spray. The F1-11s set out
for Libya. I have seen them.

I have seen the kestrel and the tree-creeper; the
sun-splash butterflies; the blue sheen on a dragonfly's
wings.

The circle of smiles ringing the pink cottages; I have
seen it. I have seen slight shoulders, stooping shoulders
sharing heavy weather.

Change-ringers stand in the tower. Clay throws up
gold. I have seen layer upon layer. And every day this
jackwind and its small rearrangements.

SPEAKING OF THE SNOW

1   *Prism*

I can see a lily spathe
and something like a moon-dog
and the globe of a tear.
Turn this face to face you
and it all becomes clear.
This world is light and what
is impossible? You may think
for one moment you have
trapped a dancing star.

2   *Snowman*

The old coal-and-carrot
routine! A wrap around my neck;

perhaps the cap of consolation.
But when all's done so damned
provisional, the work of
innocents eager to reshape
this world in their own image.
They're mainly water themselves,
and do not even know it.

3   *Lover*

I could write burning softness.
Or blinding plumage. Or fleece.
Remember Dafydd ap Gwilym:
The spume of fighting dragons.
But fleece comes nearest . . .
I could also simply say
you cover everything. The way
I see you there is nothing
that is not touched by you.

4   *Old Man*

The bright birds return to us
something of ourselves. Babies
burble, children greet them
stamping and shouting.
I watch them spin and weave,
though; I see their feathers
are frozen. In my skin
I wait, often turning
back towards the children.

5   *He Who Hesitates*

Tonight, how can I reach her?
Will I ever hear her voice

and speak to her again? Flecked
with silver: will I touch her skin?
I want her; do I want her?
This is a cage of questions.
And now? Have I already left
leaving too late? Once it starts
to snow, does it ever stop?

6   *Prisoner*

Stumps and boles and dark eyes!
There's glitter in the air,
faces at frost-windows trying
to be brave, unable to be brave.
What were the questions never
put and the words not spoken?
Walkers and skiers stream
past, noiseless, and under
the ice dead children swim.

7   *The Fair Field*

A broken army of stick-people
stumbled out of le Brocquy,
exiles on their own patch,
genderless, ageless, all of them
stiff-legged, darkened by distance.
I saw some had been weeping.
How the fair field winked and shone.
Each one, I wrote, leaned
forward with a long way to go.

BLUE WINGS

Something bright and blue and flying . . .

Yesterday a man I know,
with perfect sight,
not given to hyperbole or legpulling,
spotted a mountain-lion.

Here!
So far north and east,
after so long!

Old countrymen
ask what size
and when and where
and whether sky-blue, gun-barrel, cornflower.

They pronounce
dragonfly,
then bluebird, humming-bird, bat

and one man is doubtless right

as I who say
            for a moment
I saw in flight
the blue wings of what's possible.

SOLVITUR AMBULANDO

Left the log house with a weight on my back:
the old world, the whole world, slung in a sack
that rocked me from side to side. Couldn't stop
thinking, stop think-thinking, muttering shop
for a mile or so down the shining track.

Large as a flittermouse a butterfly
steered past me, steered and waved, sailed on the dry
thyme-rich ocean. Stepped over a beetle,
an aged scarab hammered from metal
emerald and black. The how, when and why

never bothered them. They followed their bliss.
Watched a zebra caterpillar, careless
of the rapids, a dirt-track rider,
scramble to the verge where a scarlet spider,
nothing but instinct, scaled a wild iris.

Must think, must think-think. Every inch counts . . .
But look at the hill-horse, its whisk-and-flounce!
Played seek and hide and seek with a quickstick
cardinal; rerouted a thirsty tick;
the sack began to lighten, ounce by ounce.

Tilted my hat, down on all fours, stalking:
Two deer high-tailed it, swerving and forking
and criss-crossing.
                    Fireflies danced all that night.
On one wrist I wore a bracelet of light.
I dreamed the old dream: solve it by walking.

GRACE

I left the sleepers' den;
my shining daughter smiled,
moon-face uncompromised,
first state unreconciled.

Devils danced in circles
round the tormented trees.
Boatyard pandemonium:
whips, bells and jangling keys.

Half-sightless in the rain
I waded to Scolt Head
over the sucking marsh
and round the cocklebed.

And there the ocean's guns
exploded on the strand:
double-thump and thunder,
the big boys in the band.

I watched the cormorants,
silver in their beaks.
All day alone I heard
their mewing, their fierce shrieks.

At dusk I turned for home
and I saw my waving child.
A dancer in the bluehour.
And I grew wild.

ACROSS THE WATER

In the end he did not leave us
but we rowed away downstream.
My little daughter crouched in the stern
and kept on asking. All day was dark
but that was when the clouds began
to separate, and the late sunlight
singled him out. Over the immense
purple tide we saw him leaning back
and staring up, his neck shining.
He could not hear us calling out
across the water, and my daughter stood
up. Each time we waved he waved.

GAUDEAMUS IGITUR

For the heart-shaped leaf and the mottled leaf and the
needle and the shoal shining with dew before the flame

for the dusty trunk sundered and clasped in its own
embrace the dark limbs and the lacy maze all the long fingers
pointing to the light

for the crouch and the crackle the shadow of the bleating
goat the black pig at the beech mast the bright shape-
changing mist and the dazzle of the holly spears

for the horde gyrating and the kingfisher's cry that fails
into memory the glistening wedge of granite and the packed earth

for the bronze ferns the green dreamers my children my
children at the year's turning

for the roar of the weir here and now the one river always moving
and unmoving

GENERATIONS OF AIR

I was the bellows boy. And in corners
decorated with curious tidemarks
or up against grey walls frosted with salts
I pumped and the monsters with twenty throats
or forty throats shuddered and wheezed.

Then the old sorcerer showed them his palms
and soles: they hooted and began to sing.
The last words he said to me (pulling out
from under the bedclothes not a green note
for me and a brown note for my sister,
as was customary, but his own right hand,
mottled and weedy, which he inspected
and arpeggioed across the scarlet):
That noble beast at Creake: feed him sometimes!

But in these frantic days, a mere ten years
before the millennium, most of
the menagerie is under lock and key.
The keepers no longer trust the visitors
who carry crow-bars in their handbags,
and snaffle the plate, and either cannot see
or cannot tolerate the beautiful.
And then, despite the mighty efforts

of Mrs Carwithen, and that chronicle
of practice culminating on the day
of the Coronation, my reading's poor
and I'm a poor interpreter, sounding out
the cadences of foreign tongue
I still won't resign myself to not learning.

South Creake was open, though. I stood once more
under the amused, expectant angels,

marvelling at the bourdon, the cornopean
and the oboe d'amour, and it seemed to me
the old man taught me neither team spirit
nor love of music (I honour my mother,
I honour my father) but how to listen.

Here for instance, close to Creake, in the village
where he died, beneath the raucous gulls
fishing and flying on errands, white on pearl,
I listen to the suck and drag of the creek
returning to its source, and the source
itself no more than a tremor, the sense
you are not listening to silence.

Not only to listen but to hear
myself, and come to read the signs.
To man the machine! This is what I learned –
grandfather, this and the virtues
of discipline. Always to keep steady;
to keep the beat with my left hand.
To draw deep lungfuls. Generations of air.

BLUE OF BLUE

Wild grapes!
              My fingertips are blue
and I'm alert,
cockahoop as a Viking!

Half this arboretum's blue
                              or blue.
I've tracked every page
searching for the value.

Not this jay,
              screaming obscenities,
this pair of pygmy blues;
neither the smalt eye
                        of the iris
nor the needles of the spruce, and
certainly not
                 this blatant turquoise bug.

But I'm on target!
This is the register,

somewhere
           in here
I've seen another blue,
                        more elusive
– feathered cloud, simmering,
neck of smoke
               with a blue fume
– I could have sworn it.

No racket!
          Every movement passionate,
          every word painful.
Siberian eyes.
          Somewhere in here
                           this unerring
blue of blue
with no name
           until I name it:
my fingertips are blue
                       and I mean
to entertain it.

THE LANGUAGE OF YES

This world's wreckers are at their games
and everywhere it is late.

Words words words a fury of words
hype and shred and prate,
sanitise, speculate;
they please themselves.

How can I be content
with hollow professions
or the arm's length of the sceptic?
Even with the sensory,
the pig heart's slop-and-mess?

I still want.

Let me make and remake the word
which reveals itself,
unexpected, always various,

and be so curious
(affirmation's mainspring)
I sing the language of yes.

BLUE AND RISING

'I have come to this resolution – never
to write for the sake of writing or
making a poem.' *John Keats*

White dust in my nostrils; my throat.
The track's a ribbon tossed over
the hill's back, and then it lollops
into a thicket. The only way in

to this seasoned log-cabin:
sprig of rosemary on my pillow,
acres of silence comma-ed by birds.
And now is the only place to begin.

'Your last words,' the green man says.
'Some were right, some wrong.
Bluebird? Never! And you knew it.
A false note for the song's sake.'

He strokes his Minnesotan beard.
'And knowing is not understanding;
to understand still not to grasp
what gives a rising poem blue wings.'

ELEANOR'S ADVENT
Mother's Song for the First Sunday

Which came first: word or dream?
Silver shiver on a screen,
I prayed for you and you were born.

Dumpling dancing in my womb.
Long-armed, long-legged, little frog.
I prayed for you and you were born

and I am born a second time,
my saving child-of-Bethlehem.
You are my offering; my gift;
still my loving perfect stranger.

Let me light your first candle.

December 3rd

Condensation, freezing fog, English blur.
Smoky December, that's what Martial says.
She heard a blackbird sing, and saw it surf-
and-splash out of blazing pyracantha.

December 4th

She instals herself, draped in her duvet
or her winking cat. She inserts her thumb
and her presence settles us. Four-year-old
omphalos, the world spinning around her.

December 5th

How this story fascinates her! But what
if it should change? What if the wolf escapes
next time? She will not take her eyes off it
and asks me to read it again. Again.

December 6th

Some are fruit, some flowers: Her sister is
long-fingered fern, maybe water-lily.
But she's a *compote* – no, a *macédoine*:
mulberry and plum, mango, persimmon.

December 7th

Her mother's speckled kimono: *it's like,*
she announces, and falters, wordfishing:
like bubbles what frogs make. Then they grow up.
They all change into gorgeous butterflies.

December 8th

Seeing how we hurt ourselves, and hurt each
other, she neither quails nor questions why.
Wheresoever there's a wound, she bustles
forward, shining, and plants a flower in it.

Sister's Song for the Second Sunday

Miss Eleanor Edith Sarah:
she's horrible, my sister.

On walks she whines all the way:
my path my dog my one my my . . .
She makes you say, *'scuse me 'scuse me,*
and takes my toys to annoy me,

especially my doll. She always
wants to wear a dress, even on days

when there's ice. If I could teach her
to be good, I would for sure.

Let me light your second candle.

December 10th

First snowflakes and she snubs her nose against
the glass. Light. Wet. I say it won't settle.
In lieu of last year's mighty snow-woman,
she suggests we try for a snow-baby.

December 11th

Mother: I heard you reading to yourself.
Ellie: Yes, and I'm learning to read now.
Mother: That's good. Your teacher will be pleased.
Ellie: Don't be silly! She can read too.

December 12th

Ελένη: bright one, river eyes shining
and a comedian's long upper lip.
Lullay my liking, Eleanor sweeting,
traipser and trooper, my small lollipop.

December 13th

There is a third – her little sister – and
sometimes she cries out, always beginning,
never getting anywhere. At midnight
my lost wife sweeps from room to empty room.

December 14th

Why is Christmas, daddy? So I tell her
the good tidings: silly shepherds, wise men,
a star, a stable. And Christmas, I say,
is Jesus's birthday. *Don't say Jesus!*

December 15th

A damnation of rooks, and sky so pale
blue it looks almost breakable. There's rime
on the lawn, each blade bristling, delicate:
a dazzling page she writes on, step by step.

Father's Song for the Third Sunday

I saw your first breath, breathless.
On my palms I weighed you, weightless.

Your lying so defenceless armed me.
Hearing your first scream, I sang.

In England white with ropes of blossom,
or in December, in Judæa.
Like Joseph the carpenter.
Like any father, anywhere,

crying *my daughter, my daughter,*
ich freue mich in dir.

Let me light your third candle.

December 17th

Spillikins, Memory, and jigsaw race:
she wants it understood she'll win. And when
she does, intent and pink, rosebud mouth pursed,
her first thought is to console the losers.

December 18th

Today her red-gold sister is not here,
so she controls the air-space, costume-chest,
felt-tips, VCR. She pulls out her thumb!
Easy sunlight and she sails into speech.

December 19th

As she looks, she is: Baroque *puttela*
not to be misled or lightly shaken.
Little redeemer! We nearly called her
Rosamund. We could have called her Petra.

December 20th

More ribbon, more lace, more leaping colour:
ambassadress from the courts of summer,

wearing ripe cherries; wearing whole borders!
Gardens, she says, are never quite cloudy.

December 21st

Long-lost, new-found: carolling to herself,
she claims her first brother. Locks on to him
like a limpet. And sitting in his lap,
arms about his neck, wins him for ever.

December 22nd

Sickly-sweet cloud around the sugarbeet
factory; jaundiced sun; and a songthrush
plump on the path, eyes fixed on kingdom come:
the most beautiful bird in the whole world.

Eleanor's Song for the Fourth Sunday

I saw a shooting star tonight.
      Christmas in the air!
And Jesus's birthday is tomorrow
      – what dress can I wear?
I'll sing, I'll kiss him when he cries,
      I'll brush his baby hair;
I'll bake him a birthday cake,
      and teach him a prayer.
I'll say thank you for having me.
      But . . . will he be there?

Let me light your fourth candle.

December 24th

Her quiet diligence is motherly,
her devotion Marian: unaware
she is aware of the power of love
entire. Amor! Quam dulcis est amor!

Envoi

And so she springs her box of days: hours past
and time to come. Jack Frost gnaws at the panes
but in her room a peacock stirs, flutters
to the Christmas light: momentary and sweet.

STILL LIFE: ELEANOR WITH FIELD-FLOWERS

At last the bones. After
the blazing through flamehaired
nettles, so many,
such very brief stories.
For you I deciphered them:
a timeline entire, Craske
after Craske, gone topsy
and lichenous . . . taciturn
the black stone for the
foreigner . . . and Charlotte,
taken away, 5yr 3mo 4ds.

To forget; at last to be
half-forgotten. But one,
a sailor-boy shipped home
from Crimea, was restrained
still with pale flowers.
And you, 5yr and 3mo too,
that much and a dozen days,
were so quick to protest
on this level ground at
such a show of inequity.

Lifting a double fistful
and kicking up your heels,
you ran Craske to Craske,

pelting them with stars.
One bloom tigerish and
burning at the feet of the
black Dane. You invested
each mound. To Charlotte
you came last and grave,
and hemmed her long green
surplice with rosy petals.

We did not leave the way
we came, but side by side
through parkland thronged
and breathless, along a path
quite shiny with usage. At
times you dawdled, at times
danced. Dew on the grass.
Butter light. You stooped
and pressed a field-flower
between our palms. Down to
the water: you led me out.

LEAF-GIRL

Round and round the trampled
ground between the flaming
maple and the black walnut,
and out across the nickel rink
to the winter warming-hut,
round, round with bounds and
yells, skips and little rushes
you chased October leaves.

Curtsy, shout, leap and spin,
your pale face thin and hair

haywire, the best red-gold:
so you became the leaves
you caught. And watching you
I think I thought there's
some movement, some pursuit
best expressing each of us.

A PRAYER FOR JADE

You crouching
                and eyebright
(who have an eye always
for the tiny and particular)

and over the blades
of your fine shoulders
jade combers
                stropped
and spitting
and with heaven-bellows
                        collapsing
into themselves

faint smile
            ginger tread
and you not quite
lifting the lid
of your long fingers
                    on your secret
handful of transformations

maelstrom and mill
– spill over spill
                    spraying
you with amulets

precious shower

and you unmoved
                    and still
half-bowed
intent on your fierce orisons

PORTRAIT OF A DAUGHTER

I'll draw you, my daughter,
in the shade beneath the tree,
so quiet you hear the world's voice,
so still you sense its moment.

No girl-in-the-green in oak leaves
with a passion of grass for hair,
no Rosie-round-the-haystack,
no yearning, egocentric Ophelia.

I see your head and shoulders
and whole body, nerve by nerve,
a host of troubled children,
some bloated, some skeletal.

This girl gnawing at a wrinkled breast;
this boy bawling at the empty sky;
this lump on the slow road;
this cheated meal for flies;

this bundle jolting on a cart;
this bald head; this threshing heart;
this bone-cage; this wafer;
this baby; these planet eyes.

You sit so still, you listen
so intently for each dumb child.
How can I draw you not sturdy,
not becoming as you are

but made of nothing more
than empathetic, wailing air?
Crouching hunger and dismay,
resignation seem to become you

as, taking them into you
– these poor ones, lost little ones
with only their lives to lose –
you grow into your own care

beneath the tree in the gloom.
I see you in your slow dream
learning, preparing, already near
the maze of responsibility.

Flowers you plant in others' wounds
seed themselves in you
and, looking up at me, you shine:
'I promise you. I promise.'

PEARLS AND DIAMONDS

So the Queen of the North has lost her
baubles: pearlspawn, diamond scintilla.

In the sizzling cold little bundles
reel and stagger: the angels of the artists.
First they huddle in a scrum, then they
raise their arms and squeal, and stiffen
to fall back into the flowering snow.

The swimming moon rises, and like watercarriers,
lovers float through faded rooms.
They place tulips of white light, tall,
very slender, on ledges of high windows.

On the city sidewalks families blow
bubbles, and the dancers swarm and lift
– no colour, every colour. Then each
jewel catches night, it congeals,
goes dark and silently explodes.
'Look! Look!' Mica; precious dust.

More memory than presence, a woman
drags back her rhubarb velvet curtains
and traces patterns with a shaking hand:
pink peardrops, dazzling slabs, misty
blue teeth. Is Jack Frost the thief?

(And in the city margin, a literary critic
rubs his watering eyes: the Elders
in Chelm thought that treasure had fallen
from the sky; and at another time,
in another country, another queen
with a diamond incised syllables on glass.)

Spawn and scintilla. One man turns his back
on the revelations of the midnight city.
He lies on his bed, a stone on his stomach,
and dreams about the Queen of the North.
Her loss is legendary. On the cold
white page of his mind with love
he inscribes: winter-blossom; tears;
once and future seeds; merry dancers.

WHITE NOISE

Night swallows fumes from the mouth of the stack, and dusty knots
of creeper that half-covers the brick are sealed with ice.
Lowering your voice, you talk about fireflies, all kinds of owls,
dim creatures on the slimy bed that never swim, they reach and slide.
The standard first and then seven tulips long-necked in the window:
you turn off all the lights to hear the sounds of falling snow.
All we hear at first are the animal sounds of ourselves
– our hearts' iambs, and blood whistling round our heads, our coarse
    breathing.
And snow that past midnight we scarcely see falling
except on an uptide, dancing on our window ledge, continues to fall.

Outside and shapeless, we shuffle like ancients block to block . . .
This wind's from the east: cottonwoods blossom, chastened cars
take the veil, and each cable fitting wears a busby and plume.
Motors and treads, party laughter on the doorstep, the tolling bell:
they're dampered like dreams, they sound like memories of
    themselves.
A muffler's laid over the whole huge engine of the city.

Immoderacy! I slip and drift, and believe we have no destination
and will never reach one, and that's only the beginning.
There is something white stars say to you
and you throw off all the night to hear the sound of falling snow.
As we walk the watches, still the underhum withdraws,
exhausts and conditioners, fans and vents withdraw
until in the hour before dawn there is this:
this almost nothingness;
you, floating;
the sound of silence deepening, which is white noise.

LIGHT WEATHER

To such a morning
muddied language (even the clod
of consonants) is inappropriate

– so are self-important passages,
unblinking owl-faces
and the god of the Old Testament.

Beside the island runway
the little spring aeroplanes
sniff the air.

Not a cloud in the sky,
and spry launches breeze
across the harbour

where circles and strings
of white buoys bounce.
This lick-and-spit's electric:

the lake water keeps opening
her pale hands
and flashing her secrets.

To such a morning
all our shortcomings
seem virtually redeemable;

disappointments are hung out to dry
and our shared history
is just a flawed first version.

High above the lighthouse
the ringed-bills are making
an open weave of wind.

The lake's blue shoulders
slope and bend;
I recognise this world is a sphere

and to the patient and persistent,
mindful of dream,
chance must come circling round again

on such a morning
as, flying out of winter,
you hurry to me here

and, on the island,
the willows and scarred cottonwoods
murmur in their buds.

COUNTING HER STEPS

She would still enjoy a head-to-head
with Heidegger, but not the waiting for it.
Her ardour for the sensual kept well in check
(say, chaste Lucie Rie) is no less pronounced
than it ever was, and her rejection
of the less than excellent uncompromising.
A gift for metaphor – and a sense
of humour. I can praise this woman!

But anxieties make her hoarse: her health;
the whole estate of her children. Her hair
is silver and ash, and downy as a cygnet.

Today she told me that on her constitutional
– and all day golden rods and storm clouds,
charcoal and indigo, and swirling leaves –

she counted her soft steps. One by one.
'Two thousand three hundred and ten,' she said.

True, she went on to ruminate on aspects
of the mile, beginning with the stride
of the centurion. But how easily she tires.
She sips and sups no more than a sparrow.
Is this how she begins to simplify:
counting and recounting the sum of her steps?

CLAY, SYLLABLES, AIR

*In celebration of the life
of Dick Crossley-Holland*

> not is
> past tense
>
> past time
> and warm
>
> tears are ours
> this spring
>
> and lemon
> morning

Let us make a man from syllables.
I say his eyes will be sapphire blue.
You were going to say the same thing too.
I say like David – Michelangelo's –
he'll have long arms, long legs, big toes.
You praise his proportion: head, hands, feet
and say he'll make a fine athlete.

We can agree and disagree;
prediction is like this, and memory.
Let us make a man from syllables.

Let us make a mind, let us make a heart.
You say he'll do right and never great wrong.
I say he'll always sing the right song
or stay silent: what I call natural grace.
You say he will be brave, and face
all weathers with equanimity.
I say true teacher; kind and witty.
You say a man who will love his wife,
his three children – who will love life!
Let us make a mind, let us make a heart.

And we will invest this man with air.
A subtle compound. I say he'll need
a mouthful – a sailor's daily creed
brought from mid-ocean. And you say smoke:
ring upon ring of Gitane, a blue cloak.
I say that mix of salt, iodine and mud
– let Nelson's air, Burnham air, sing in his blood.
Then may this creature of clay inherit
rushing breath: the holy spirit.
And we will invest this man with air.

     morning
     and lemon

     this spring
     tears are ours

     and warm
     past time

     past tense
     not is

FROM THE HALL OF THE AUTUMN PRINCE

How can I stand the cicadas?
Raucous as the dead.

I see a silver needle of air
above my head.
It will spiral through my fontanelle.
I shall not go mad.

When . . . when I . . .
gristle in my throat.

When I become king
I shall legislate against the past
and sanctify the new.
The court will be convex
and I shall be surrounded
by inventors and babies.
As soon as a woman has suckled her firstborn
her nipples are to be shorn
– likewise the testicles of the father.

No one in the kingdom will be
as old as I am.

Bodies are to be burned,
ashes scattered.
Headstones will be forbidden.

How can I stand these cicadas?
I will have them netted and boiled,
all the dusty pines they squat in
are to be hacked down.

Do away with the sidling lizard
and its wicked ancient look.

I shall not go mad.

How many?
How many days?
There is shame in waiting,
the hot wind hisses
the same words again and again.

I will discriminate
against all likenesses
and comparison and memory.

Nothing is to remain of him.
Let the shrieking birds
carry him and his shade
out of the kingdom, high over the waters.

He is dead already.
This is the kingdom of the dead hand.
Hollowed steps, withered olives,
and all the little rancid shrines.
Husks of ritual.

I will do away with his foul dispensations.
He chokes on his own obsequies.

Cicadas. Cicadas.
I will keep my years young
with what's new and disposable.
I shall not go mad.

Scrape the ground clean of shards!
Roll out the shocking pink
when I . . . I

THE FOX AND THE POET

Please tell me please. How chancy is it
For a young fox to meet a hungry poet?

A poet! It's time you were properly versed.
Of all our enemies the poet is the worst.

Worst! I thought poets were just amorous,
devious and gaseous, penurious – but glamorous.

They're shape-changers. They dream and devour.
They translate you and take away your power.

Don't tell me please. If he catches me,
What will happen if some poet bandersnatches me?

You'll be locked behind words. Cribb'd; confin'd.
Howling you'll run to the limits of the mind.

TRANSLATION WORKSHOP: GRIT AND BLOOD

Hige sceal þe heardra, heorte þe cenre,
mod sceal þe mare, þe ure maegen lytlað!
Word-stand, locking shield-wall
not to be broken down, nor even
translated in its own bright coin.
Courage, intention, resolve – won't do.
Out with Latinates! I want earth-words,
tough roots: grit and blood, grunt, gleam.

Harder heads and hearts more keen,
spirits on fire as our strength flags!
Here lies our leader, axed and limp,

the top dog in the dust. He who turns
from this war-play now will mourn
for ever. I am old. I'll stay put.
I'll lay my pillow on the ground
beside my dear man, my loved lord.

THE VIKING FIELD

Not only thistles.

Gossamer: a shining network
woven before dawn.

Obstinate couch-grass
tall and blond
manning the ditches

and roses
tougher than they look,
craning their necks in hedgerows,
pale, shallow faces
following the sun's arc.

Scent of stone
and basting clumps of cow-dung.
Good warm glue.

A crinkle of silver foil
in the far corner.
Blind eye
flashing like a field of broken ice.

Day's breath bated.
Grass growing. The sound of it.

Sound of wool
growing on the lamb's back.

Systems of ants
stream out from their quarters
to inspect the field.

And even now
no dragons are forecast
for tonight,
but the candid sky
begins to congeal and sag.

Clover.
Wild garlic.
Ragged, unscrupulous crows.

Lance-leaves and heart-leaves,
tawny hairs, stinging.

Then all these spirit-wings:
this flickering assembly,
each silent woman flying
on her own
double-headed axe.

THE OLD MONK: VALLE CRUCIS

Under Fron Fawr
the wings of our old sycamore
whirligig again –
they're brittle and brown.

Huge carp skulk in the underworld.
The whole stew's alive
with glides and grins.

Saturday night
Brother Garmon and I
saw the floating bones
of Sister Linnet,
we heard her white skull singing.

Fron Fawr.
Almost half her green skin gone.
Purple for a season.

When I sit at this grille
the mass of the beetling hill
wholly occupies it.

Look at the sheep
perched on the escarpment:
dun and bright,
in and out of sunlight.
Look at the crown
and the rumbustious clouds

toppling over it.
I've grown so old and
it's halfway to God.

THE ALDEBURGH BAND

Somehow a mouth-organist
has got into the flue
of the gas stove in the Baptist Chapel.

Every minute or two
she draws a plaintive chord
that dies as the north-easterly
roars in the stack
and the blue flames leap.

But it's in the gazebo
painted star-white,
all the benches wet with mist and fret,
that I recognise what's happened:

when the timpanist plays hide-and-seek
and beats his tiresome tom-tom
in whichever cubicle I'm not,

I soon see or, rather, hear,
the whole ragged band
is billeted piecemeal
around Aldeburgh.

So, for instance, the fat man
with the alpenhorn
has found his way into the massive
stone head of the sea-god –
Aegir, president of the flint-grey waves
– and he keeps bellowing in my ear
every time I pass him.

There's a pretty lutanist
behind that lattice window
on Crabbe Path;

whenever she leans out,
she runs her light fingers
along the modillion.

And the contralto with the treacly voice:
there's no escaping her!
She's always under sail, beating
up and down the windy High Street,
decked in globs of amber.

But where's the maestro
– some say magician?
Is he locked in the foundation
or under the long-eared eaves, still
tuning in?
The Aldeburgh Band:
did he have a hand in this?
Those who tell don't know.
Those who know don't tell.

Darkness comes in to land and I walk
along the beach
past the very last silent fisherman
with his lantern
and ghostly-green umbrella.
Crunchcrunch under my feet. Crunchcrunch.

Down to the water's edge
and still the music's everywhere:
all the strings night-bathing
and phosphorescent,
playing glissando;

the stray with the cor anglais,
lonely as a whimbrel
over dark water;

and far away,
far under the glagolitic ocean,
the now-legendary player
of the tubular bells.

EAST, WEST

Pity the fool, poor frantic,
crossing himself over mid-Atlantic.

No time to win on either shore,
he's unable to give more than more.

He frequents apparent light,
and translates depth as height.

Looking east while looking west,
for each is better, and both best.

ANASAZI WOMEN

And with whichever story you come,
from whichever quarter or time,
the signs here mean the same.

Rock, clay, how they speak to us.

And as if from pink-brown pouts of cliff
snake-tongues of water
have slipped down, dripped down

and passing through themselves,
running through string-thin runnels,
the narrowest canyons of their own making,
grooved the high mesa, every limb:

shin-deep,
knee-deep,
thigh-deep,
hip-deep.
The passage of feet feet feet
rubbed away this white rock.

Women of clay,
sooty-lunged,
fingertips and palms
spiked by cactus,
how could they make these tracks?
Were they so blade-ankled
and slender-hipped?

Pots on their heads
heavy with hominy, pumpkin flesh,
were they so high-stepping,
knees to wasp-waists, each foot
placed directly in front of the other?

On this neck
high above the talus and twisted cliff-rose,
one petal of flint,
milk-white and deadly.
And look!
A sandal of crushed yucca leaves,
fringed at the toes.
Soft footfalls, fit for spirit-roads.

Women of clay, bearers of water.
Abalone in the sunlight.
Sweet song
of the wingbone of the golden eagle
crossing time.

And up top, as if the bandit wind
wields some giant rake with silver tines,
all the scruff and hardscrabble
is striated,
and scrub oaks rasp.
And where wrens flute
and loop,
the ground is stiff with sherds
– not sloping shoulders, slender hips,
not the little feet of dishes or fingerdips,

but all that remains
of pots proud-breasted and wide-hipped,
pot-bellied pots like melons and gourds,
ample, kind and porous.
Cream slip,
black slip,
orange on sepia,
mouth wide, womb-wide,
round as this poor planet
we make, and break.
How gently she rocks the globe
in her net of hair.

And the women:
bones of the women,
carters of corn and buffalo-fat,
hordes of gnats
gyrating around them:
all misshapen, ricked by arthritis;

their shining teeth
are ground down to their gums.

Neither tall nor slender,
not lanky as foal or fawn,
but thickset, short, stalwart:
poor imitations
of their own healthy pots.

Women of clay, Anasazi women.
High-stepping
through passage and cut,
crack and cleft
up and down from the windy mesa,
they left a dancer within warm rock.
Her feet tap, her fingers click,
time has not turned down her smile.

And there is a piper
lifting life's music,
replaying it to heaven.
Rock-woman, earth-woman,
coiled, almost foetal,
almost ready to spring out and stand,
singing-and-saying
and and and

SELF-PORTRAIT

Thin white line and knot
on the forehead, quick to flare
– a medal conferred by a croquet mallet
on the upswing fifty years ago.

Nose tipped with a spare piece of putty.
Thistlefield of a chin,
highly competitive.

The folds of the eyelids
confidential, not quite epicanthic.
Ears almost Carolingian!

Eyes expressive; always inhabited.

Mouth shapely, concealing a canine
capped and painted in subtle tinges
- milkblue, oatmeal, cucumber flesh –
by a Bavarian dentist.

(Look! A face is a face.
What did you expect?
This quality, that defect
– the whole bag of tricks?)

Expression in repose: somewhat worried.
Professor from the cradle
with a silver head
tilting forward, a little to the right;
an earnest of concentration.

IDLING

The way waves fold into themselves, sigh, then
play themselves out high on the foreshore,

a man draws and redraws the crescent contours
of the salt-woman he loves to draw to love.

PUPIL

Way to go the same way I went yesterday.
This way I see more: each blackberry,
each Norfolk reed – more plump, less plaintive.

Way to stare into the world's eye and see
its quick reflections; the pupil of now.

TO THE EDGE

To the scatter of a hamlet where nothing happens,
slowly. Sixty generations banked in the mud of
dogged minds.

To the scruffy hem of a rhomboid: acres torched and
charred. And far off as childhood the boy with
Punch and plough now a man astride his scarlet tractor.
Trawler of a torque of yelping gulls.

To the bounding lane. Skimmed and lumpen. Spinning
balls of gnats; matted honeysuckle. Acid in the
elderflower, old-fashioned Albertines athwart an
unhinged gate: those were the days less happy than
we think they were.

To the empty paddock and salt-crusted wall, the glossy
guarded holm-oaks.

To Mother Creek, flowing and flowering: her Byzantine
dark fingers laying open the marsh. The pools and
pulks are orange and sepia and slate-blue. Silt. Salt.
Yap of rigging. All the old arguments.

To a spur that's ragged. Beyond the leaching chemicals
and uprooted hedges, to the crossing-place where soil
and saltmarsh meet.

To a floor of uneven flagstone, filmed with beeswax.
Unfounded. Well-trodden. Flanked by clods of flint,
rough lime mortar.

Look at sun's fierce lances, the dance of light on
stone: word and spirit have reached an agreement.

The smell of mud and rose. You know you can still
tune this world: the way the mind infiltrates, ideas
assemble as if of themselves; the heart's pluck;
ancient, inner voices.

To an innocent page, damp and salty, and this fitful pen.

To the edge that's always chill and uncomfortable.
Tall reeds sing in the ditch. Tide turns against
the wind, bucking and amber and hilarious.

FOUR CAROLS

1   *The Nine Gifts*

I bring you my body, darling dear:
My ripening song, my jubilant ear.
That's what Mary sang. *Alleluia!*

And I bring surprise – this sweetest fragrance
Made with love and hope in patience.
That's what Elizabeth said. *Wonder!*

I come with a trill and a blue light
And followers stumbling through the night.
That's what the star sang. *Rrrrr!*

Well, my lamb, I've got you this fleece
So your old mother can get some peace.
That's what the shepherd said. *Yan! Tan!*

I bring you the broken tooth of a giant,
No compromise, the word that is silent.
That's what the stone seemed to say. (   )

I bring you guffaws and loops of mist
And a band of brown hair for your right wrist.
That's what the donkey said. *Eeyore!*

I bring you my crown and an uneasy dream
Of duty and honour, gossip and scheme.
That's what the king said. *Heigh-ho!*

Open your hand for this fitting glove:
The name of the song in my throat is love.
That's what the ring-dove sang. *Coo-oo!*

But what can I bring you? I bring me.
Whatever I am and all I will be.
That's what the child sang. *Little Jesus!*

2   *Pilgrim Jesus*

Iesus! Christus! Iesus! Natus!

In the manger of my body
Leaps the tiny child, and his breath
Is the word – the dance of God.

Corpus! Beatus! Peregrinus! Natus!

In the ocean of my head
The steadfast ship rides tide and storm
On its pilgrim crossing.

Oceanus! Peregrinus! Christus! Natus!

In the orchard of my heart
Springs the singing tree. Its root
Is faith and its sweet fruit charity.

Cor! Arbor! Amor! Christus!

Riding ship, springing tree,
And in the manger leaps the child
Who is the word – the dance of God.

Iesus! Peregrinus! Iesus! Natus!

3   *The Heart-in-Waiting*

Jesus walked through whispering wood:
'I am pale blossom, I am blood berry,
I am rough bark, I am sharp thorn,
This is the place where you will be born.'

Jesus went down to the skirl of the sea:
'I am long reach, I am fierce comber,
I am keen saltspray, I am spring tide.'
He pushed the cup of the sea aside

And heard the sky which breathed-and-blew:
'I am the firmament, I am shape-changer,
I cradle and carry and kiss and roar,
I am infinite roof and floor.'

All day he walked, he walked all night,
Then Jesus came to the heart at dawn.
'Here and now,' said the heart-in-waiting,
'This is the place where you must be born.'

4   *Jesus, Springing*

I am the heart that houses the cone
I am the cone enclosing the cedar
I am the cedar sawn for the cradle

forest of the body
body of the tree

I am the cradle rocking the baby
I am the baby containing the man
I am the man nailed on the cross

tree of the body
body of the forest

I am the cross sawn from the cedar
I am the cedar enclosed in the cone
I am the cone housed in the heart

here in my heart
Jesus, springing

LIKE A SMALL SIGH

Along the thin line
            of light under your bathroom door
I see your cat stretch and bow down. She makes
strange little noises deep inside her throat

until you admit her to your steamy sanctum.
That is the first I know of today
except for snow ploughs grinding and cackling
like a skyful of rooks
opening the frontiers
between night and morning. I am half a dream away.

With right hand, left leg, I claim your side
of the bed. The sheets are warm and silken.
Then it's the spit-and-flush of your shower,
wrapping me, pre-natal, until as usual the Nutrigena
slips from your slick fingers and hits the deck.
You say as soon as you step out the cat jumps in
and laps and licks the whole tub dry, every drop.
I can understand that.
                    When I open my eyes
again, you've reassembled in our little bedroom.
Naked sylph wearing nothing but a white turban,
little more than an outline in the feeble
light beginning to leak between the slats.
You are so narrow at the hips.
                         You bend, I can
scarcely see the groove between your apple-buttocks.

Disciple at a dark drawer, you fuddle over what
and mainly what not to wear: this white, that black.
No, white! Now over them your silk magnolia slip.
Such care; such hesitation.
                      What is more doubtful,
more lovely to watch than a lovely woman, dressing?

5.30 exactly and the telephone rings
                              – not a fax
from England, as happens often, but quick fire
from a friend: the roads are too icy; freezing fog;

or freezing rain. Yup! Your school opening's
delayed for two hours.
                              You whoop me up, and then
at once you penguin down the passage to the kitchen.
Not listening, I listen to your ancient
radio's crackling confirmation: Saint-Croix,
Catholic Springfield, Sauk Center, Stillwater . . .
Another call, another colleague and a second volley.
'I'm back to bed,' I hear you say.
                              Incautiously,
you peel away your silk skin. Ribs of white light!

You enter the bed like a small sigh,
and still we've exchanged not a single syllable.
At first you turn away, hook your left ankle
over my left heel.
                    One breath! You dream yourself
deep into curves, almost imperceptibly.

AND GOD SAID

My work! It is so beautiful
And they did not realise it.

So I made monkeys of them,
Tipped loads of morning duty over them,

Turned the knife in their sides until
Each petal of blood was unbearable.

                    ***

I hurt because they hurt me:
They could not see me clearly.

So I put into their eyes the gauze
Of morning mist in the valleys

And a double measure of pain. Still
They cannot see me clearly.

***

Syncategorematic! How clever they think
They are. True, I will not strip them

Of my word, but they keep wrapping
Themselves in words of their own.

Thousands of beatitudes, millions
Of platitudes stand between us.

***

But sometimes the scales fall from
Their eyes. They stare at green hills,

Their swelling breasts, and indolent clouds
Stooping over them. Innocent again

Of all they perpetrate, they dream
And almost know what I intended.

***

They are not just one of my rehearsals
And each day they grieve me.

How they bleat and snort and bray
And lay one another's mates.

Nerve gas, bombs, land mines!
I was right to fix their term.

***

During their dark season trust went
Into hiding: they wrote thoughts on air

And tried out their own nightmares.
Some were needed for crocodile meat.

But I have given them generation.
A few I have ennobled to say no.

***

I have bandaged their wounds with illusions.
They think their hurt is mortal,

They believe their suffering improves them
And are convinced they can change nothing.

They say I have told them
They will live again after they die.

***

I see poets – a whole unreliable army
Of egotists, promiscuous and unstable.

I am the yeast, I am the priest,
I am the alchemist, I am the conscience . . .

Listen to them! Do they really
Think they will have the last word?

***

How they go on searching for me.
Like lovers on love's threshold

They stare until their eyes burn,
And suppose they almost see me.

As if I were hiding from them
– gargantuan, dressed in skirls of cloud.

***

Taut nipple, shocking pink stem,
Loops and ropes of indigo and flame

And scarlet blossom folding in
On itself: all this before leaf-rattle,

The mouldering and dung beetle.
The fools! I gave them eyes to see.

***

Let my children hear each speckled leaf
Sing a song no less singular

Than their own. Let them enter
Into understandings with water and earth

And each unblinking stone.
Are these not ways back to me?

***

They are so powerless, so afraid
Of knocking night. Look how they sow

Seeds of stammering light
Halfway up the flank of the dark mountain.

– Ah! Had I not chosen I would
Still choose to assure and shelter them.

***

Where they are, I am.
I will always prevent them.

And whatever looks into their eyes
Will divine their song without ending.

But I will release them. How can I
Deny them the mercy of time?

***

Who watch the crying world wide-eyed,
Without averting their gaze. Who keep

Faith through the fatal night.
Who accept all they think they cannot change

But move when they move with the rhythm
Of purpose. My own children!

***

What opposes grace? Disgrace.
And brutality? Tenderness.

How can hate mother love?
What is the distance from no to yes?

They live in these interstices.
I live in all their choices.

***

Sometimes I think I did not dream it
Entire but only in night's shallows,

And say I have always failed them.
Sometimes I gaze at the curvature

– such shining, such darkness –
And believe that this is still my dream.

***

I watch how they deceive themselves
And deceive one another.

Since they have cast me in their image
They suppose they can deceive me.

And because I have set them free
They cry I have deceived them.

***

They test me with their anguish,
The fearsome hound of their hunger,

Foul diseases that disfigure them,
Worst, their sullen armour of indifference.

I cannot turn them away. Like them,
I change nothing. I suffer their suffering.

***

There is another darker dream
I cannot contain. Is it because

I have chosen not to come close
To them, or because they are not constant,

Or because of their wild beauty,
I trouble myself I am their dream?

LIMOGES

All I knew of Limoges was my mother's china:
teacups transparent as raised communion wafers,
with knuckled twig-handles, their gilt half-worn.
Shining bone miracles tough as old boots.

When the night train pulled in, quacking,
it was damp and chill. One frail old woman,
coiffed and frilled, peered out from her kiosk.
Hooded eyes. Top lip stitched. Time to kill.

ANASAZI

Where altitude snags
                    our breath
pink rocks writhe.
They scald our fingertips,
and she-pines underswish.

This is where she gasped . . .
and he fired spirit-arrows . . .

We cannot quite run these people to earth,
least of all by turning over each stone.
Even written words weigh much
                              too much
when ruins are so little more than
rearrangements
of the place's bones.

Here is the human abattoir . . .

Up against their overhang
vultures catch thermals.
How hungry they are
for life, cresting
             and swooping,
hurrahing through groves of gamble-oaks,
cinders in the valley.

Orchard of little peaches …

So where is the song
of that hidden bird
             leading us?
Canyon wren?
We are not even sure of its name
but have come to recognise the tune.

Curious and careful,
             we are here,
and they know we are.

from SWARM AND HONEYCOMB

in memoriam Margaret Douglas-Home 1906–1996

II   *Saints of the Foreshore*

Who hum among bee orchids, wink and
wilt again with each wilting sea campion.

Who heard the German Ocean rasp, and suffered
draughts, damp cold and like punishments.

They grew into ground, stay-at-home pilgrims
drawing near with faith in the company of seals

and avocets; partners in stubborn understandings
with thrift and anguished hawthorn-trees.

Rinsing ascetics at the head of foundations
and kindly teachers of knock-kneed novices;

contemplatives islanded in their own cells,
distillers of sweetness, harvesters of God.

Celtic mothers and Saxon fathers: their piety
most enviable because uncomplicated,

though hard-won. But who said anything
should be easy? Not the crusted stanchions

on the foreshore, nailing together earth, sea, sky.

III   *The Wellspring*

Infant of the bubbling spring
well in my heart.

Child of the sighing marsh
breathe in my head.

Son of the keen light
quicken my eyes.

Rebel of the restless creeks
tumble in my ears.

Disciple of the rising tide
dance in my heart.

Teacher of the gruff salt-wind
educate my tongue.

IV   *Half-Saints*

Near as a heartbeat yet foggy and far
one bell swings in the high tower.
One heart beats and a modest crowd of folk,
some of them strong and all of them weak,
make a bee-line for church.
                              Collectors
of small change for good causes; doctors
of the heart; dependable helpers
who befriend the lonely; stitchers and quilters;
two Samaritans, not quite anonymous; makers
of church marmalades; aid-workers on leave,
leathery and haunted;
                              few of them known
outside their own communities, none heroes
or victims, but singular women, singular men
who expect the arduous and mundane
and avoid plaudits.
                      Lives of the spirit!
Bees circle them as they sleep.

V   *Crossing-Place*

This is the house of the unspectacular
and invisible;
                  the threshold of some dream
or of something we once knew.

Kingdoms of the earth, sing to God.

This salt-bleached tower!
Who conceived it and who ordained it?
Who hired the master-builder and was he paid
on time? Who blessed the quoins?
Who moved the stone?

Kingdoms of the earth, sing to God.

Pulpits, rood screen, Virgin in outline,
acanthus leaves:
                        one gift for love
of God, another in memoriam;
this one a matter of appearances;
that, down payment on a passport to heaven.

Kingdoms of the earth, sing to God.

To step inside time
by answering the pulsing bell
our grandparents heard
                        and seeing stars
of sunlight at play on an ancient wall
is one way back, and forward;
to sense worn hands and lives
in fabric visionary or homespun
is to cross the threshold
                        scalloped by love.

Kingdoms of the earth, sing to God.

SALT-COMPOUNDS

salt-scythe
sweeps onshore, corrosive and hissing; pins back
ears; rifles each stay, shroud and halyard.

creek-wood
the old ones, clinker-built and always thirsty;
noses blunt and bottoms glaucous; still quivering.

sea-garment
roseate spinnaker, light-breasted; no less
stiff canvas, often split and mended, grey with salt.

herring-haunt
see-through escarpments toppling and barking
as they dive through themselves into ghosts of flint

mauve-mist
delicate as breath suspended over marsh grass;
summer carpet, wiry and tide-beaten, knotted in mud.

wave-arms
without joints, creaking and groaning; like wings
their strange spade hands salute and dip and rise.

mud-runes
ribbon-casts, blow-holes, keel-scrapes, anchor-spikes,
darts of the stitchers and strutters and mincers.

THE GRAIN OF THINGS

Beware of what's uniform, lapidary, slick.

As if a twisting country lane
where shadows bow and curtsy

were to be avoided
because of its green spine and blisters;
or it were desirable
that literary translations should not sound
foreign and close to the originals.

Waxen-skinned fruit is apt
to taste less sweet than the pocked potato
and ruckled pomegranate.

Let me have about me
not members of the awkward squad
or fools so cussed they cannot compromise,
but friends who think, and say
what they think, not given to repeat
themselves with variations;
men and women with robust wordbanks
who deal in things no less than intuitions
and cast their cloaks before the beautiful.

Salt-milled stone has its place.
Oil has its place.
Likewise the assembly line.

And no, I have no wish to be abraded
when I am low in spirits
or to listen to the litanies of the bigoted,
nor even to be pricked by the moustache
of an amorous woman!

But give me the gruff,
the honest stumble and crux –
the obstinate knot in the grain of things.

THE ART OF PICKING BLACKBERRIES

Containers seldom grow on trees.

***

Follow a hedgerow centuries
old. Hawthorn-and-lime, ash-and-sycamore
link arms, and through its bright windows
you glimpse once upon a time
– no more than a breath away.

***

Some berries are hairy; some have scabs;
some are perfectly formed but exceedingly small.
The juices of many taste diluted.
Choose refined but vigorous stock.

***

Be so peaceable the pigeon
attentive in the thicket
does not fluster.

***

Never wear gloves, like some murderer.
Expect purple thumbs and forefingers.
Expect blood.

***

Gather them still almost firm when
very gently you squeeze them:
those that come
away from their stalks a little reproachfully.
Embodiments of sweet asperity.

***

Victorian families of ten or twelve.
Fourteen!
But the firstborn grows misty, already sagging soft,
while some of the bunch are still rosy-cheeked,
and the little one hazel-and-green.
How many is it right to pick from one cluster?

        ***

n.b. And how many papulae,
this rounded, that faceted,
glisten on the body
of each berry?

        ***

Bindweed and nettles! Bryony and nettles!
Risk the sting and overreach
for that best one
you almost catch exposed and off-
balance.

        ***

Ignore the reticent sloes
(that gin still squats at the back of the cupboard)
and the punchbag hips
(chemists used to buy them: fourpence per pound).
Keep away from haws.

        ***

Now to extricate this hedge.
This one berry.
Fleeting breath on your cool brow;
yellow light; plumpness;
swollen fingertips, a little numb, not quite your own.

        ***

The art of picking blackberries is
to know when to stop.

MOORED MAN

Moored Man's Song

His feet are caked with creek mud,
his shins are indigo.

And yet Moored Man lifts his eyes
across the slakes, across the waste
and sees an island, riding.

His arms are tied with marram roots,
his thighs strapped with green weed.
He wears a fraying halter.

Moored Man lifts his grey eyes
and peers through iron-cold bars.

Colours of salt and honey.

He is half-old, tide-worn, wind-worn.
He roars and starts to sing.

Moored Man Almost Remembers

Sheen-eyed and unblinking, quick
to the creek's sudden lurches and quivers.

Undergrowling
at the far fierce crash and pound
deep day makes sullen.

Before all this.

Did he fall?

Was it a hundred wings with one will
raised him into air-tides?
When he swam and drifted. When he cried.

At dawn he rises from the groyne
under the barefaced sky.
His forearms shine and ripple.

Once more he braces his blunt thumbs
and sinks them into boulders.

One blue window in his mind.
One feather tarred to his left shoulder.

Making the Island

Why?
Because it welled up – a single keen wave
out of the flatcalm of his mind.

He squelched and splashed north.
He waded out
a mile and more
up to his thighs, his hips.

Why?
To see felicity.

On the hazy bar he began.
With both feet he scratched and scraped
like a wild sea-cat covering its faeces,
until his ankles were bloody and raw.

Then he kicked. He kicked.

Why?
So the Polar reach
would end in his ears?

The gravel flew and dropped,
it swarmed and swirled like chaff
in the murky water.

Longshore drift did the rest.
Pebbles and grit swam
and settled in new stations.
They rose above themselves
out of the water.

Schschschhh-huh!
Soft echoes in the cavern of his mouth.

Time and wind.

A shining cap of sand!
Sea-kale, tugging at its roots.
Sea-holly, growing beautiful
as it grows old.

Sss-sk! Sss-sk!
He strikes sounds on his sandpaper tongue.
Sss-sk! Tt! Tt!

The sun draws its blade
over his welling land.

Why?

Because it was not there.

He stares at his island
and knows he is beautiful.

Young Woman

He begins with her toes.
One by one
by one he massages them
and paints them silver-blue.

He applies indigo poultices
to her porcelain ankles.

Then he shows her his claws.
Scratches her shins all over, very lightly,
until she stands shivering under midday sun.

And kneels to him.

The further she comes
the more he grows towards her
and reaches out behind her.

The backs of her knees:
he tickles them with a feathery wisp.
And then he wraps himself around her skinny thighs:
bleached pink, lavender.

He is waiting for her at the hanging valley
and the dark pool.

She stares at herself in him.

Instead of a Roar

First he sees everything, then
narrows his gaze
to nothing but his fierce intention.

Three lolloping, laughing boys,
each blowing mist balloons
and stuffing them with loud words.
The point of his silence lies in wait for them.

Next, the retriever walking his chapped mistress
and grinning:
for one the slip,
slime and mud-slurp for the other.

High on the dyke's shoulder
black pods rattle
and late bugs trundle over lank grasses.
The parcelled woman with sore eyelids
stumbles, sobs.
Wasteland of my heart, she thinks.

He is like the barn owl:
pouring out of himself upwards
and very fast, quietly
spreading the dark sheet of his shadow.

One disciple stands his ground.
He watches Moored Man for months; for years;
He sees through him.

Foreigners

Where are they always going?
Why are they coloured yesterday and tomorrow?
Foreigners!
Why do they have so little to do with him?

They goggle at him through binoculars
and chuck empties at him.
They swear at him and shit on him
because they cannot see him.

Moored Man is still glad, though.
He likes how they look,
and their looking at each other.

He likes his dreams.

When dark clouds laced with silver
gang round the sun
and shadow-ribs race away across the marsh
into the mudflats,

he sobs inside himself again,
unblinded and knowing
how they must have to do with him.

Waste

When they hurry through, eyes cockleshelled
against the savage light,
declaring they love him and what would they do
without him,

and how all summer

he was benelsoned
like Lady Hamilton's breasts,

and how his groynes
need more attention

all their words are only for themselves
and each other.

His heart aches.
His ears start to sing.

He watches three curlews work sobbing water,
he inspects the massive spar
dressed in stars of salt
with rot in its gut.

His bones – are they melting?
One day he feels almost weightless,
the next he sinks back blue
into himself,

and he broods
until the tide turns in him once more
and he could rise and ramp
before the howling wind
and blot out everything.

Unknowing

Pear and pale pink and oatmeal
 – he can see for miles
the southern rim breaking
into colour,
flaunting spring flags.

He can hear the taunts of golden trumpets,
and the piercing cries of children,
and young lovers sighing in their bones.

So pitted and pocked.
So invaded. So exhausted.
What is he
today but an old grey map again
crossing itself?

Moored Man grinds his heels. His teeth.
He cannot help himself.

He stamps
and his mud splatters the sky's pane.

He thumb-stops his ears.
Crouching, he sees nothing
for hailshot, for hot tears.

Moored Man's Plan

He sleeps with a stone on his stomach.
When he wakes
he sees the upshot waiting for him:

crabs will sidle from their shells,
lobster pots turn themselves inside out,
mussels will play their castanets;
buoys will harness themselves in weeds,
saltwater and freshwater
will stand up and embrace.

What a dance!
Snub noses bucking, clinkers slipping anchor.
The price of disrespect.

First he must cock his ears.
He must listen
deep into the sound
of the sound where all sounds meet.

Next he must make of his own throat
and diaphragm a winding marsh-horn.

Moored Man's yawn: it is whale-wide.

The third thing. The third
will be the third thing
will…

Whale-wide; cloud-wide.
Again he falls asleep.

His Voice

Growling as he sleeps,
his own sinking world's ground-bass.

His voice is like the memory
of gunnery practice out at sea.

Dark brother
of the swill and pound and chatter
way beyond the cockle bight,
ocean's mouth
ancient and still promising
to deceive.

Witness

While he peels off his tatters, sodden
with dew, and tosses them into sky,

his tern flaps and hovers,
its javelin scream
white as the edge of the first morning.

What does he see?
A looming impression
in the creek's murky obsidian
and the flashy mudflats?

Can he see himself at all
in the green shoots bristling on the marsh,
the leprous rashes of sea-pink?

They see him.
They bear witness to him.

Naked he stands,
upright
where restless levels meet:

tall as a sun-lance,
a bright column striking,

while on an air-stream
his tern balances.

Ablutions

He begins to stretch through himself
– his daily becoming.

Sharp blue teeth; flounders and flatfeet;
sudden sloshing.
Then the crook-necked grey one
Stabbing and gulping.

He stares at his skin's asterisks –
salt-crusted scars,
spatters of flowers like service-medals –
and lets each tide rise through him.

Once again the ruckled beds and lays
go under, and the soft mound, silver and grey,
around the freshwater spring.

Each day he rises,

and over his head
the light grows fearsome.

Trickster

As though he were the son
of apparent light and the mimic jay:

he quivers and glares,
he unrolls carpets of sticky mud,
then spits laughter as he laces
fine sand with pointed stones.

And as though he were screaming quicksilver:

he rises to the moon,
drags the lumpen tides
until the creek's swollen and impassable . . .

But tricksters turn to darkness.

He licks oozing blood,
rubs salt into wounds;
he cracks and snaps bones.
In the evening he drowns little children,
and then he howls with remorse.

Old and wild and angry,
child of mayhem,
father of grief.

The Same Badge

When they inhale his minerals, their blood
fizzes. They soon grow giddy.

Standing on a mudslide spit
a young leftie casts his line, slips
and barbs his own right thumb.

Their slates are too good to lose.
Two boys playing ducks-and-drakes
skim them across the narrow creek
straight at one another's shins.

Now someone's daughter leaps
from Old Stoker's wreck,
drives her incisors through her lower lip.

Each summer victim wears his badge:
a ring of stinging iodine
around the leaking wound's mouth.

Before the Storm

What is on its way, massing
upstream, is like a tower about to topple
or a cloak of spelter bruised with purple.

And what is smooth-ironing
the afternoon's long sleeve
is his own stillness. Effortless his water
swans down midstream, softly
it backheels in the margins.

Each minute hangs and seeps. It trickles
through his myriad gorges of mud.

Birds cross very high, out of earshot,
and balls of gnats ferment
while still he dozes,
one glassy eye open,
until his sheer shine could blind you.

Storm's gonfalons hoisted and advancing,
Moored Man unhurried but at bay:
this perfect equilibrium
arrested
on the shield of the waiting day.

His Shadow, His Smile

When her own quicksands
snagged the woman on the foreshore
and, choking, she did all she could
to clutch her left breast,

Moored Man trembled until
his bone-joints cracked. His teeth ached.

Laser gulls tacked into the headwind,
shrouds and halyards keened;
low he stooped
and threw his long shadow over her.

Stopgo shrimps soon sized her up.
Come whiskers, come pincers!
Come terns and cormorants!

She was his golden cornstook,
she was his wave-cornflower
until the jade tide turned and made,
and beckoned her.

Gently Moored Man smiled
as the pale sun blinks and smiles
on the stranded and the breathless,
on the dark wave's welling
and winter wheat.

Searching for the Stone

On seventh days
his labour is to search for the stone.

He turns his back on the comfortable bells,
the silk-and-velvet cattle
stamping on each other's shadows.
First to comb the foreshore after high water.

Although it is there
it is never there
at first, and then as no more than a glint
in the corner of his bloodshot eye
He rakes the shingle beds beside the creek,

glares until each stone turns sepia.
Until pebbles crunch his brains.

And then
it is there.

Utter,
transparent and unblinking.

Between his rough fingers he holds it up.
He raises it,
free and shining,
quite clear of time.

But he knows what he has to do:
he draws back his arm,
hurls it, slings it
into the water's throat,
as far from him as it has always been.

Moored Man's Tides

He faces the offing and world's rim.
home of the nightfall.

This bickering and sucking soft, this
lapping as tide grows heavy in itself,
then dies to be reborn:

how does it mean? How do tides mean?
This falling and rising,
moaning and thrust.

In his gut the puzzle bubbles and ferments
but still cannot surface.

If only he could spring it –

The welter; the rim;
the colours of separation;
always the ache of his tides
chiming
deep within.

Her in Him

He sees how she spreads herself.

The scallops of her palms,
the little blue hollows.
Her ribs – their pale crescents and sparkle –
and the clippings of pearly razor-shells.

Her salt-stiffened sprays of green hair.

Ankle-whip, shin-whip:
she wears skirts of wild silk
slit to the thighs.

Soft, stale O of the hagstone's mouth.

Each night the cold white flames
of the slakes and oozing meals.

Ghost-Light

Under the Milky Way
his hidden lips and little throats
open, they stay open
as he sips and gurgles.

Under the dark, burning spaces
he spreads himself and plots himself.
Prone and accepting.

He strops his blades
under the red star.
Like nerves his wiry hairs quiver.

Under the wrenching moon
he is slats of ghost-light,
he is ribs and rising.
All he is, all he was
in this dream of re-becoming.

Quite

No one knows.

Or, rather, everyone knows
but each tells a quite different tale.

Moored Man listens.
He sleeps with one eye open,
gauzy with death-mist.
He who hears the artillery
of popping bubbles, beetles tap-dancing
and the shooting scooters,
listens.

They were home on leave.
They were Home Guards.
Foreigners.
They were Germans.

Both men were wearing identical uniforms.
At Bank Hole, beside the groyne,
they stripped, or did not strip
but the sea stripped them, naked.

It's a day's dive to the bottom.
Diz with her webbed fingers and webbed feet
is the only one who ever touched it,

unless they touched it.
When the whirlpool dragged them down.

What of their stigmata?
Snagged, gashed on a spar's nails.
No! Drowned men split and tear.
No! They clawed each other.

Moored Man listens
until they are quite finished.

All everyone agrees
is both men were found floating,
they were lolling
side by side, moon-faces up.

Saying

Saying:

I had forgotten as the old forget
this morning's deep charge:

plumbing each orifice,
gouging scum from my veins,
bursting my pockets.

All my pus and jetsam!
I will usher it
into the marsh
where now filters into then.

Saying:

I turn, I make, I flow, I come.
I also am young.

His Line

Headline. Heartline.

Line from once to will be.
Innocence to responsibility.

His skyline
murmuring
to west, to east.

His line about you
and now
if not always.

Marooned Man

Is this it?

Nothing barking; or breaking;
no chitter-chatter.
Nothing in the spire-shells of his ears.

Amongst the reeds of the freshwater creek
the chugging coots make not a sound;
neither does the sizzle of gnats.

He is cocooned and cannot see himself
in focus, only that he's dressed
in shining, sticky webs.

The gut's half-drained and listless.
His limbs are limp.
Nothing's bated.

Is this how it will be
– this erosion of the senses, and exhaustion,
one long ooze?

His skin is drenched,
his arms outstretched.

Yet he is smiling almost,
still alive, marooned, and unfree.

IN THE WINDOW-SEAT

Because of the knot and Soutine swerve in the grain of this pale oak;
the slim plank's wide hips, its fit and quiet sheen;
because of its ancient wounds;
and all the veins in the greenstone, and the notch gouged in one corner;
because of the warbled panes which cannot see straight;
because of the hot eyes of the marigolds;
the rising trot of the horseman who never draws closer and never goes
away;
and the moat that corrugates and comes out in goose-bumps;
because, hearing, you cannot be heard; and, seeing, you cannot be seen:

I believe that, after a long courtship, with customary decorum;
still too shy to be at ease, at the start of a suffocating afternoon;
and in haste, with lace still wrapped around one ankle, trousers
    half-dropped;
I believe that young and delirious, wistful, seasoned, culpable;
padding out this bay with pillows and bolsters;
fingertips sliding from skin to pane, digging into the soft cames of this
    latticed window;
in this sweet compartment;
I believe that fruitful, and with disastrous consequences, and with no
    obvious consequence at all;

as you;
as you and I;
on this common board between cradle and coffin;
first with your legs dangling over the side like a puppet's;
puffing your lower lip, cockleshelling your eyes;
and then; at last with a long sigh;
small silver heels wedged against the riddled beam;
while the moat still dreams, thick and green, and ring-doves moan.

Because here a dragonfly settles on my right shoulder, not quite unafraid;
I believe;
as wraps of mist rise, and it is clammy evening.

OCEAN PATHS

I am crossing an ocean for you

and by whatever route and means I go,
direct or long and stopping, quick, slow,
the crossing will be slow.

I should have expected it.
A boy, I took short cuts into cul-de-sacs and deep water

and, a young man, I thought matter no match for will;
I still half-hope for the quick fix.

On the tossing northern route blue helmets howl,
the mother whirlpool grinds men's bones to salt,
and arsy-versy corkscrews twist people up and out beyond gravity.
The southern way's no better; it undermines all resolution.
Mist whitens your pupils and oozes into your brain,
it assails each cell with soft self-doubt.

Onward! Back! Sideways! On!
Voices of air and ocean swill and hammer
until you know only you cannot distinguish them.

I am crossing an ocean for you
and there is no easy way to cross an ocean
the way you cross a kitchen, a lawn, a leaping hill.
I must risk the risk I will not reach you.
B-bubbub! B-bubbub!
My old heart keeps singing in triple time.

Before I am finished, I may be a good Lutheran...
Flushed and gagging,
I will insist I want nothing easy,
nothing worthwhile comes easy,
Lord! Could be I will learn to suffer gladly.

But this way or that, you still prove me,
and guided by homing lights
transmitting their warnings and far-reaching promises,
by degrees I find myself
astonished by love.

YEARLINGS
for Nigel and Sue Cox

Sleep in a heap through the heat of the day.
They prick their ears at dusk, gangling rise,
tear off and jam on the brakes
halfway out across Two Furlong field.
Ranged in a horseshoe, they stamp and huff
and uproot the plump May grass, forgetting
quite what brought them here to begin with.
Youth's so quick. Nothing troubles them
for much more than a minute, nothing
escapes them. The moment one sheep
squeals next door, they're on their way again,
craning their lean necks right over
the hawthorn hedge to inspect the reason.
All evening they're on the go, white blazes
whiter in the gloom, racing to and fro,
quartering the field with their questions.
Very late, there's a light-show and,
catching each other's almost-terror,
they career along the foaming hedge
to the far corner ribbed with barbed wire.
So soft-eyed. So mystified.
They are languid, edgy, elegant
and, after midnight, grow so remote:
vague clouds crossing inside the skull,
shadows of something far off, long gone,
we would have done better not to have lost.

HARE

Hare knows green road and quiet lane,
hare knows well-beaten track
are best byways there and back
though her headlamps are set crooked.

> *Cat-of-the-wood and cabbage-patch stag,*
> *squat-in-the-hedge and frisker.*

Advances within herself at a slow lollop.
Stops to sniff the brisk northeasterly,
stiffens, pricks her pantomime ears,
makes off at a fair fine wallop.

> *Sit-still and shiver-maker,*
> *snuffler, twitching whisker.*
> *White spot and lie-low-by-the-dyke,*
> *boxer, little busker.*

Senses me, believes in me
– everything I and my kind can become.
With pad-scratch, sideways skelter
vanishes into long grass, fields almost golden.

> *Wide-eye, wall-eye,*
> *witch, dew-tracker, trickster.*

Except she's never anywhere else
but only where I fail to see
and just when I do not know:
at my elbow always, wherever she is.

BERNARD

1

More, much more than touchstone:
omphalos, almost,

still-centred and unshaken
at your end of life's table

presiding over whatever
your family and friends bring to it

– all our glosses, small successes,
dropped stitches, little deaths –

one day terse or waspish,
the next sweet as sixpence,

whole-hearted always,
true as a compass trembling.

That long table is one
of Norfolk's high hills,

book-bouldered,
stacked with papers,

where clutches of wildflowers
cling to precarious ledges

and bagels and bara brith
shelter in the crevices.

Carla's kitchen, yes,
where body and spirit meet:

I think of it
as an ante-room to Eden,

the tendrils over the sink
reaching out to their garden sisters,

all the watercolours
in states of dress and undress,

(rehearsals, really)
and always the tide's surge-and-scour,

– greetings, laughter, small talk,
empathy and argument

deepening into meaning;
reluctant goodbyes.

At our feet bottles and Wellington boots,
baskets, a bucket of cockles.

Around our shoulders
the Aga's warm wrap,

aromas of cumin and cinnamon,
cassoulet, quince cheese

– all these, Bernard, and your encompassing,
well-nigh seraphic smile.

2

Well back from the business end
with its zipping lasers,
its bodyboards and lycra,
I walk and wade

to the snub of the creek
where a pair of scruffy herring-gulls
(both have seen better days)
pick and peck in the slake,
and what was once the island ferry
is tethered to a slime-green stake.

An ancient couple perch
on a concrete wall, legs dangling,
so long together now
they've lost much need to speak.
There's no one else about
except the usual suspects
– Buchan, Belloc, Williamson –
beating the hotel bounds,
revisiting the Moorings.

How easily the two of us
could have become close friends,
each with word-fever,
each tender, and possessed
of a sense of humour,
both with Burnham in our blood.
For this evening at least
I'll set aside our shortcomings,
and just sample your achievements.

Item: the novel you published
when you were only twenty-four.
Item: the students who loved you.
Item: gourmet and clam-gatherer,
journalist and editor, radical…
More than this, much more:
your reading so warm, so wise
– the way you see through,
and often see *into*.
So much I've aspired to.

Is it true
we never once were night-bathers,
young gods together
in this mud-cake and reek
when, maybe once in a year,
the tide on the make
becomes phosphorescent
and each dash of water shines,
each limb is luminous?

Did we take a wrong turning?
Was there some mistake
or misunderstanding?
Not that I can point to.
I came too seldom. You went away.
And you were three years older.
Quite simply, the friendship
others thought might happen
fifty years ago did not happen.

And has not until now.
Bernard, we've said so much
between the lines
of these last weeks, these seasons,
and we can tell so plainly
all that's lost and won.
We too are on the make
as I turn from your bedstead,
and walk and wade,
and write this ache.

SALT-BRAMBLES

Where sound sluices
through that gap in the dunes
salt-brambles glisten,

they sparkle, though northerlies
scorch their leaves
and cancel our footsteps.

Pick one, all the others shudder.
Drop one and they're eyes,
red and black, moist.

(Remember those that peel away,
that lollop softly inside the bush
well beyond reach.)

If 27 love-spots
is the best answer,
what is my question?

So tart their juices your mouth
puckers; so trickling sweet
at the back of your throat.

Salt-skinned, their blood hectic,
so quick to flow.
Your lips look a little swollen.

THE PATIENT WIFE

Green dawn. That plane in my Summer Courtyard
with parakeets shrieking among her cool hands
has entwined her tall companion with gossamer,

her spiders have spun high-wire crossings,
thousands of silken strands, dewy and shining,
much more strong and supple than they appear.

He is her guardian. He overshadows her.
She's well-used to all his airs and heartaches,
his limb-secrets on long nocturnal journeys
lit by glow-worms. She is his sweet binding,
his seeress, undulant. He is her lattice,
her swoosh of laughter. Her column of tears.

I can see how she is spinning him home
from wherever he absconded last night
which she feels not the least need to know.
And he can see how she is playing him
with her weaving and waving, her enticements,
and I believe she believes he is glad of it.

HAMMERSHØI

Where there is brightness, it's always beyond,
on the other side of the wide window
– and so, by inference, before or after,
anyhow elsewhere. She waved her wand
and banished it all a long time ago.

A long time, is it? She scarcely knows.
To and fro she rocks, to and fro,
waiting while silence advances on us
and we see what she sees indoors
and out, stealthy as falling snow.

Where's that pin? She was holding it between
her bony fingers just a moment ago.

THE MOUNTAINS OF NORFOLK
in praise of sugar beet

Monstrous clamps of the great unwashed!
Grubby little Audens, dwarf-hippopotami
of the green kingdom. Each one's the sum
of its own prehistory. They smell rank already,
not like rotten trout glowing in the dark
but rubbish we forgot to chuck out yesterday.
Talk about the mountains of Norfolk...

Chalky cephalopods, their suckers and tubers
thick as penises. Grizzled old groutheads,
some scalped or shorn like combatants,
some with bristles wound round their waists.
Warty misshapen tubs, this with several snouts,
that the hooded eye of a giant tortoise.
Here's a head with the grin of a gaping shark.

Not one of them has aged beautifully.
They're like foetuses cropped from milky wombs
unformed or malformed. Boxing gloves
with knobs on. Very much more heavy
then they can possibly be. Horny, lacerated,
inescapably coarse. Not one has ever
dreamed a wild dream or seen an angel.

These thousands of stubborn brothers,
pitted, pocked and jaundiced, on a dark night
you might want to avoid them, all hunkered down
against the roaring body-snatchers.
Soon the bubbling pyre. Soon the sickly pall.
When at last the foul shall be beautiful,
and they too become authors of sweetness.

AT THE JOCH

Far below
they kicked at muddy papadums
and their doe-eyed children scrunched
and balled and hurled them, squealing.
They shivered at the indigo
overhanging them, and quaked
at the violent bellow-and-growl
they heard moments too late to witness
the avalanche. They have submitted
to layers of unknowing
and raised their eyes
to one sunstruck pitch, unbearably bright.
But nothing has prepared them for this.
Here on a slatted deck above the silent world
they stand about in shining mist,
raise their arms, bend back slender wrists,
cup their hands as lotuses,
like supplicants awaiting entry to heaven.
And now they cry sweet soft cries,
smile blissful smiles.
Turning to each other, they murmur, murmur
as very little pieces of white sky,
thousands and thousands, drift down
and touch them – their noses, lips
and eyelids, their fingertips –
gifts of clean water and quick light,
glistening white crocus,
six-pointed stars.

CHUNTERING

You're always chuntering. While you propel
yourself around your kitchenette, debating
which snack next; while you're inspecting
the myriad channels, and with little
shuffling penguin steps heading fast
for the deck where you take a dim view
of the ice-blue weather. As if word
makes flesh. As if word drives your heart.

Often, your patter dovetails now with then,
and your mnemonics summon companions:
yesterday's nurse, cautioning you not to fall,
not to fall, and the state trooper warning
'youths will shoot you as soon as look at you'.
Also Pastor Nelson, God's narrow spokesman
– but above all your pit-prop, wise and warm,
icebound for two years now at Fort Snelling.

Several times each day you begin to giggle.
You giggle and gasp, and then announce
you really don't know why. Because you've seen
it all; because whatever's not unbearable
has become absurd. Fortified by small
essential household wonders, and rosy,
unshakeable in your faith, you laugh
until tears stream down your crumpled cheeks.

BEYOND WAS TO WILL BE

Act Four or Act Seven,
they amount to the same thing:
time for the oldies to perform
before the curtain comes down.

Some friends have disappeared
into the dark already.
It can't be helped. At least
the survivors are present and correct,

but sitting in the front row
they feel exposed and do look
rather leprous, though they're pleased,
to have room to stretch out their legs.

The second and third rows, too,
catch one edge of the harsh light
intended for the stage, and they're peopled
with plenty of familiar faces.

Four rows back, there's nothing but shine
– pupils and thick lenses,
foreheads and tips of noses.
It dazzles the oldies. Their eyes water.

Further yet, they discern
heads without features, padded shoulders,
almost shapeless shapes, darker
than the dark breathing around them.

And that's the end of it.
Beyond here, no faces, no limbs,
no identities or even masses.
The oldies keep looking, though,

staring and searching for presences
they know to be there,
the ancient ones, if anything
attentive and benign.

Their voices are cracked
 and ten points north of east
 – not one of them can sing
completely in tune –

but they're well on their way now
beyond was to will be,
and most of them are laughing.
They know the piano knows the song.

BREATHLESS

The barn owl holds our breath,

– contemplatives peaceful
as lily-pads, having learned
to bottom out and fathom the world,

transformed now into pilgrims,
stricken almost by this first sight
of the one we've longed to see.

In this easterly bluster he balances
on a stanchion, perfectly aware
we're observing him ignoring us.

With vast unhurried wing-sweeps
he rises silent above himself,
hangs on nothing, sizes everything.

All his days a readying for this
moment when he gathers, swells,
swoops behind the hawthorn hedge

and gives us back, breathless.

RISING

And on all sides
always
lie the fields
of flint
– another million
surfacing
each night
from the chalky soil,
keen light
knapping them,
oatmeal,
grey-green, ghostlike
as waves breaking.
Flashing
dragon's teeth
of these salt-acres
where first
shall be last,
while hidden
beneath the last
of the last
sings our song
always,
shines our gold torque,
turns the key
to our hill-house
of green
words rising.

HUBBUB

for all the hubbub and the blather,
and the tyranny of choice

which way from babeldom
 to syllables of sound
– each tone of the heart,
and the brain inch-inching
along the path of reason?

for all the ease and do-as-you-please,
the pick-and-mix smile and voice

which way from cradle and breast
to the sheer crossing-place,
the battleground
wound in dark veils,
home of the hard-won?

for all the creeds and dusty screeds,
the hand-me-down and the decreed

which way, like a novice
eager to unlearn,
from will to willing
and that shining emptiness,
the cloud of unknowing?

for all our doubt and self-doubt,
our seasons of drought

which way from yesterday and tomorrow,
to one song
wild and soaring,

still unsatisfied,
here, now and for ever?

for all the hubbub and the blather,
for all the ease and do-as-you-please,
for all the creeds and dusty screeds,
for all our doubt and self-doubt

one song wild and soaring,
here now, now and for ever.